LORD,
SAVE MY MAR
or
SAVE MY LIFE!

THORNCROWN PUBLISHING

LORD,
SAVE MY MARRIAGE
or
SAVE MY LIFE!

SABRINA R. BARFIELD

Printed in the United States of America

Published by:

Thorncrown Publishing
A Division of Yorkshire Publishing Group
7707 East 111th, Suite 104
Tulsa, OK 74133
www.yorkshirepublishing.com

Cover design by Jay Hughes

Text design by Marlon Villadiego

Library of Congress Cataloging-in-Publication Data
Barfield, Sabrina

ISBN: 0-88144-350-6

For licensing / copyright information, for additional copies
or for use in specialized settings contact:

SABRINA R. BARFIELD
strongtowermin@yahoo.com
www.sabrinabarfield.com
www.strongtoweroutreach.com

Book Dedication

For all the hurting men and especially women who are calling out to the Lord for direction in their marriages, this book is for you. I've walked in your shoes.
I know that God will answer your call.

"Fear thou not; for I am with thee: be not dismayed; for I am thy God: I will strengthen thee; yea, I will help thee; yea, I will uphold thee with the right hand of my righteousness."
(Isaiah 41:10).

—⟶⟵—

This book is also dedicated to the single men and women who are trusting God in receiving God's best.

Table of Contents

Acknowledgements

With Special Thanks:

To the Lord: I give thanks and honor to my loving Lord and Savior. He trusted me to write this book [to you] at one of my lowest points in life. Through my struggles, the Lord gave me the strength and the ability to tell my story.

"I will serve you all the days of my life. I love you Father."

To my children: Thank you so much for your support and understanding. I spent so many days and nights shut up in my room. Thank you, Beyonka, for your dedication and support in watching your younger sister. You both mean the world to me. I love you.

To Angela Davis: An "Awesome" woman of God. Thank you for your spirit of excellence. As my editor, I could not have chosen anyone better. You have an ability to hear from the Lord, and you allowed the words of this book to come to life. With the Lord's guidance, you made this book possible.

To the morning Oak Cliff Bible Fellowship prayer team: During the process of writing this book, I faced many challenges with my health. It was the morning prayer team that stood up and prayed for me without hesitation. Thank you for allowing God's promise to come to pass.

To my mother: You have been great. Thank you so much for your prayers and believing in me. I could not have done this without you. You are the greatest mom. I would not trade you for the world.

To my sister, Tam: Thank you for remaining patient with

me as I continuously harassed you for direction in writing the book. Thank you for keeping it real. I love you!

To the brave woman who shared her testimony: I applaud you. What you shared was not easy. It was challenging for me to share my story. So I do understand you had to die to yourself so someone else can live. Because of your honesty, many marriages and lives will be set free. May God continue to bless you!

To my best friend, Cynthia Daniel: You have been with me from the beginning to end, the pits to the palace. Through all my struggles, you never judged me. You only showed me love. When I needed a shoulder to cry on or someone to listen, you were always available. Thank you for being a true example of James 5:13-16 (NIV), "Is any one of you in trouble? He should pray. Is anyone happy? Let him sing songs of praise. Is any one of you sick? He should call the elders of the church to pray over him and anoint him with oil in the name of the Lord. And the prayer offered in faith will make the sick person well; the Lord will raise him up. If he has sinned, he will be forgiven. Therefore confess your sins to each other and pray for each other so that you may be healed. The prayer of a righteous man is powerful and effective." Thank you for being a true friend and a real sister. "I love you so dearly."

Last, but not least, I like to thank a woman who inspired me to accept God's call to write this book. I met this young lady one day when I was at a clothing store called Ross, near Robins Air Force Base in Georgia. As I was in the shoe department, and I was humming a song called, "Praise is What I Do." A woman looked across and placed her eyes on my eyes and asked me softly, "Excuse me! What are you singing?"

I responded, "Praise is What I Do."

Suddenly, tears began to fall from her eyes. Immediately, I knew something was going on in her life, so I decided to sing the song aloud. I sang "Praise is what I do, when I want to be close to you, I lift my hands in praise." Then she said, "I am about to start crying. You just do not know. You have made my day. I have been going through so much, and I really needed that."

I discovered that she was having marital problems. She had been married for almost 20 years and recently found out that her husband was having an affair. Although, her husband was cheating on her, she decided that she was not going to give up that easy. She was going to fight for her marriage and depend on God for restoration.

After she had shared with me what was going on in her life, I told her I was experiencing a similar situation. Then I told her that God had prompted me to write a book on marriages. She looked at me and said, "I'm waiting on your book. I'll be looking for your book."

I do not remember this woman's name, but I pray that God granted her request and restored her marriage. Wherever you are, know that I will never forget you and because of you, I accepted God's call to write this book. "I love you."

Foreword

It was a great pleasure to read Sabrina's book entitled, *Lord, Save My Marriage or Save My Life*. Ms. Barfield is a powerful example of the grace and goodness of God. She chose to express this reality through the tool of writing. I love that this book both encompasses challenges and rewards. Sabrina was unafraid to use her personal testimony to help someone in need. To me, this is one of the greatest measures of character that exists. This book will radically express her passion for the presence of God and her greatest awareness of her need for Him. One's life experience is one of the most terrific expressions of God's love and comfort.

It does not matter where you come from or what you are going through if you know God can see you through it. I highly recommend this book to anyone who is facing tremendous obstacles. Our obstacles do not define us, but how we overcome those obstacles do! You, as the reader, can gain incredible insight into the life of someone who was willing to lose it all to gain something much greater in God!

Amanda Conner
Director
Destiny Leadership Institute

Introduction

There are men and especially women who are living in abusive marriages and do not know which way to turn. Some have accepted physical, mental, and emotional abuse as a lifestyle, and some have even died in the wilderness because their lack of knowledge to the Word of God. In the Bible, the prophet Hosea received a word from the Lord to give to the children of Israel. He said, "My people are destroyed for lack of knowledge." What you do not know, *will* hurt you.

I pray that through this book you will gain knowledge about which direction the Lord wants you to take. As I was going through my own struggles, God inspired me to write this book. It is amazing that as we face trials in our own lives God causes us to minister to others through our own pain.

When God gave me the vision to write this book, I had no idea what would be the outcome of my own marriage. Many days I wanted to bail myself out of the marriage and call it quits. However, I had to learn how to trust God and hold on to His Word without letting go.

When you die to yourself, someone else will live. At first, I did not want to share the personal things about my life. I was afraid of what people would say or think about me. Then God said, "Are you writing this book for Sabrina or for my people?" In other words, "How can I bring someone out of their present situation if I'm not willing to share my past?"

These words reminded me of something my Pastor said during one of his messages. "If you knew half of the things about the person sitting next to you, you would get up and move!" In most cases, we never know a person's past or what

God has brought them out of. We tend to forget the day God brought us out of our situation and placed us in His glorious Kingdom. He did not do it just for you, but He did it so you can help someone else.

This book has changed everything. I never wanted others to know about my secret life of selfishness, pain, hurt, shame, and struggle. For you, I'm willing to share my testimony. The pain and suffering I experienced in my life is the last thing I want for someone else to experience.

It was through prayer that God gave me the vision and the purpose of this book. In a dream, the Lord told me "I am the voice of one calling [*crying out, shouting*] in the desert. Make straight the way of the Lord" (NIV, emphasis added). These words spoken by John the Baptist prepared a place for Jesus Christ to enter into the hearts of broken men and women. Now, I have the opportunity to call out to the many men and women who may be in the wilderness asking each one to open your hearts and mind to the voice of the Lord.

Know that God has not forsaken you. There are some of you who are barely holding on, refusing to give up and trusting God for direction and total restoration. On the other hand, there are some who feel they must accept the situation because God hates divorces. For whatever reasons or questions you may have, I pray that as you read this book you will receive your answer from the Lord.

You will see my story through the eyes of my childhood, how and why I got married, the suffering I experienced in my marriage and how I drew closer to God through my experiences. My childhood experiences had a great impact on my decision to pursue a marriage that was not ordained by God.

Sometimes, when we go back to the beginning of our lives, we can understand how and why we got into our present situation. We do not use our childhood experiences as a crutch or excuse to justify behavior, but we can use it as a point of understanding emotions and responses to various situations.

Before you make any decisions, I encourage you to read this book and sense the leading of the Holy Spirit. I believe that God will order your footsteps in your marriage day-by-day until He gives you an answer. It is through your patience and obedience will you possess the promise (Heb. 6:12).

THE PROMISE

1

IN THE BEGINNING

When my mother got a divorce, I was 10 years old. That's when I found out that the man who had been married to my mother was not my biological father. For all of those years, he was the only father I knew. When I found out, I was torn apart. How do you explain this to a 10 year old child? All the excitement had come to an end. The man I once called "Dad" is not my real father. I could not understand why my other two sisters were still receiving gifts, and I was not.

After my mother's divorce, we moved to Meridian, Mississippi. That's when the pieces to my broken puzzle came together. Once we arrived in Mississippi, my mother told my sisters and I that we would be living with a woman called "Madear" until she could provide for us financially. That is when I found out later that Madear was my real grandmother and her son was my true father.

Madear pulled down from the wall an old dusty, antique

picture of a dark-skinned full sized black man with bifocals that almost covered his entire face. Madear looked me directly in my eyes and asked, "Do you know this man?" Without hesitation, I said no. I had no idea who this man was. I had never seen him in my 10 years of living. Madear looked at me as her bifocals sat on her nose and said, "That's your father." Immediately, I told her that was not my father. Madear said, "Yes it is." I knew it wasn't wise to argue with Madear, so I respectfully said, "Yes ma'am".

This was one of the hardest moments in my life. It was really difficult for me to grasp. Thinking of the man my mother divorced, "How can someone be your father for 10 years and then the next day he is no longer your father anymore?" For many years, my heart bled with anger and resentment. A total stranger that I just met told me something that I would have rather heard from my parents.

Sadly enough, not only did I lose a father, I lost my aunts and uncles. I felt so lonely and isolated. Everyone knew about this but me. My sister, Tam, tried to console me, but that only made matters worse. Since they divorced me, I felt it was only right that I divorce them. That same day, I adopted my new family name: Cook. This name belonged to my grandmother's (Madear) family. I felt I had to start all over again and win my approval from my new family. They lived totally different from the lifestyle I once lived. I went from suburb living to a wild life with no structure. For instance, I was told that a Cook woman does not allow another woman to take her man. If someone takes a man from a Cook, then you were not a true Cook. This was my new life, and I had to live up to the family's name to be accepted.

As a result, I started having sex as a teenager. It did not matter if I was hurt or completely disrespected by a man. I had been released from a man who I thought was my real father. What could hurt me more than what I had just experienced? I had a new father, and his name is, "Father of all lies." You got it. Without knowing it, I turned my life over to the enemy. I carried the hurt and pain of losing my father for many years. A huge void was in my life, and I was trying to fill it with my lifestyle. It took time for me to realize that only God could fill that void.

I was saved at a young age, but I was definitely not living a saved life. I confessed with my mouth and believed in my heart that Christ was Lord of my life, but I did not change my lifestyle or renew my mind to the Word of God. I continued to live like a hellion. I was exposed to clubs, alcohol, and promiscuity. The club became a second home for me. I lived there from Wednesday to Sunday. Before I could get home, I was already back in the clubs!

I continued to live this same lifestyle even as I joined the military. It was obvious there was an emptiness I was trying to fill. I have a friend who always uses the cheddar cheese analogy. He explains how cheddar cheese has many holes. He uses this analogy to address how individuals walk around like cheddar cheese with many holes in their lives. The problem exists when we do not allow God to fill those holes. Instead, we find other things (sex, fame, pornography, drugs, alcohol, relationships, clubs etc.) to fill the voids in our lives. I tried filling my voids with unhealthy relationships.

Mr. Right

In August of 1997, I was stationed overseas on a short tour assignment. When I got the opportunity to leave for the States, I spent my time in Atlanta, Georgia with my cousin Samona. I met Samona when I moved to Mississippi, and we both lived with Madear. When I arrived at the Atlanta International Airport, Samona was waiting for me with a big smile and a warm hug. From there, we went to her house where she lived with her brother and his friend Jack. As I was unpacking my clothes and getting situated, Jack, standing 6 feet tall, lanky, and barely weighing 140 pounds strolled over in my direction and approached me and said, "You're very beautiful, and I'm attracted to you." Every day while I was home, he would remind me of how beautiful I was and that he wanted to be with me. All of my life I waited for someone to love me and acknowledge me, and here is Jack doing just that!

So we ended up talking more towards the end of my leave. He seemed like he was a good guy, so I continued to listen to him. Before you knew it, I did it again. I found myself having sex with Jack outside of marriage, committing sin against my own body. That was my first mistake. I barely knew him. I cannot give you any explanation of why I did what I did. It was just a lifestyle that I learned at a very young age. As a child, I watched my Aunts live this kind of life. Now, as an adult, I was acting out the things I learned as a child. It seemed like my aunts had men, but no intent of staying with them. Still today, my cousins would repeat what my grandmother said, "All men are dogs, and you cannot trust them." We accepted the lie believing there were no good men. As a result, we moved quickly from one man to another to avoid any hurt.

Soon my leave had come to an end, and it was time for me to go back overseas. I said all my goodbyes, and I was flying back across the waters to a third world country to do the last half of my assignment. In a year period, Jack and I talked twice. We did not have much communication at all. Finally, it was time for me to leave and go to my next assignment, Lackland Air Force Base in San Antonio, Texas.

REDEDICATION

My mother use to visit me quite often in San Antonio. It never failed; my mother would always pressure me into going to church. However, I did not go to church much at all. I would tell my mother to leave me alone and let me live my life. Although I rebelled most of the time, she never stopped asking me to go to church. She was determined to get my life back on the right track. One day she asked me to go to church, and I finally gave in. She asked me to go to Cornerstone Church, Pastor Hagee's Ministry, in San Antonio, Texas.

Early that Sunday morning my mother, daughter and I got dressed and headed to Cornerstone Church. That morning Pastor Hagee preached an awesome sermon called "Your Barley Field". It was so powerful that it literally began to change my life. The Barley Field represented something special in your life. At that time, the most precious thing or person in my life was my 12 year old daughter, Brenda. I had Brenda right after

I graduated from high school, and she was very dear to me.

As Pastor Hagee continued to speak on the Barley Field, he stated that God wants us to choose Him before something drastic happens in our lives. He gave many examples. The one I remembered vividly is the one of a father who never went to church. The father had bought his 18 year old son a red sports car for his birthday. That night his son and couple of friends went out to celebrate his birthday. Sadly to say, this was the last time his father spoke to his son. His son had a fatal accident and died immediately on the scene. When his father received the news, he was devastated. After his son's death, he began to go to church. It was the first time that his father had ever picked up a Bible and went to church. He now reads his bible and goes to church faithfully. I remembered Pastor Hagee saying that God wants to get our attention before he removes something precious from our lives. During this service, I walked down the aisle and rededicated my life to the Lord. I was in the right place at the right time. Pastor Hagee preached directly to me. I was a single parent, and I had one daughter at this time. What happened to that young man I did not want to happen to my daughter. I definitely did not want God to remove her from my life because of my harden-heart and transgressions. Therefore, I gave my life to the Lord, and I began to live my life the best way I knew how with the little knowledge I had of Christ. Of course, it was not an immediate change, but I was on my way to becoming a better person. I began to go to church more often, and I started falling in love with God.

Shortly after I rededicated my life to the Lord, I heard that Jack had moved to Austin, Texas, which is approximately 70 miles from San Antonio, Texas. It had now been 3 years since

I last saw Jack. Jack had moved with my cousin, Melvin, to Austin. They were friends since childhood. Wherever you saw Melvin, you saw Jack. They were inseparable. They had recently moved to Austin looking for better job opportunities and both working as electricians. Somehow I got his phone number, and we began to communicate again. It was not long before I went to Austin to meet Jack. We picked up where we left off 3 years ago. The same as before, Jack started telling me how beautiful I was and how much he loved me. Only this time, he wanted to marry me.

Now since this was three years later, I was at a point in my life where I desired to have a husband. It seemed like everyone was getting married except me. There were times, I felt like something was wrong with me. I considered myself to be a beautiful and an attractive woman. So where is my husband? I was almost 30 years old, and my husband had not arrived. I figured either God wanted me to be alone or He somehow looked over me. I felt like my biological clock was running out, and I needed to get married…soon!

I believe a lot of singles desire to be married before they turn 30, and if they are over 30 then they feel like something is wrong with them. Well, that was me. I no longer wanted to be single, and this would be a good way to not have sex outside of marriage. Since I had rededicated my life to the Lord, I wanted to live my life right. As a baby Christian, I thought this was the right thing to do and maybe Jack was sent by God. Although, I never had an opportunity to know Jack, I was excited about the fact of being married. Pre-marital counseling was not even a thought. I did not understand the biblical side of marriage. I thought our decision to get married was God ordained. Later on, I found out that it was not. That was after I established a true relationship with God, and He was able to remove the scales from my eyes, and allowed me to see the true person that I married. Unfortunately, it was too late. I was already on my way to a marriage that almost cost me my life, my children and my ministry.

There were many road blocks, red flags and warning signs, but I did not recognize them as an infant in Christ. The first sign was when he continued to tell lies over and over again. First, he said that he wanted to marry me, so I prepared for marriage. At the same time, I found out from one of my uncles that he was telling another young lady the same thing. He was lying to the both of us and living the better of two lives, some may say. I was really upset about this, so I asked my sister to ride with me back to Austin, so we could get to the bottom of this. When we arrived to Austin, I could not find him. I had asked my cousin where he was. At first, my cousin denied his whereabouts. Eventually he gave in and told me where Jack was. He told me that he was over at the other girl's house. He took me over to her house. I began beating on the door and asking him to come out. I made up in my mind I was not leaving without an explanation. That particular day I believe I woke up the entire apartment complex. I was filled with rage and anger. I believe I had so much anger I could have killed him. Thank God they are both still alive today.

I was so confused, and I demanded an answer. Jack finally answered from behind the locked doors and said that this other woman was holding him hostage and would not let him out. At the time, I really believed she was holding him hostage. I called the police and waited for their arrival. The police demanded that she opens the door. Finally, she opened the door, and he came out. For a long time, I believed the lie Jack told me. I truly believed that she held him hostage, and he could not get out. Again, I was so naive about the whole situation. Later, I realized she was not holding him hostage. Jack had lied all along. I believe Jack assumed that I would walk away quietly and leave the apartment complex. He had no idea that I would go to the extent of calling the police.

Demanding to get Jack back is from the behavior I learned in my childhood. That is why it is so very important to do a self-evaluation of yourself and your childhood. You can then determine why you do some of the things that you do today. Without realizing it, I was living up to my family name. Remember, no one takes a man from a Cook. What would my family think if this other woman takes Jack from me? This would be an embarrassment to the family name. I had already lost one family, and I did not want to take the chance of losing another one. I found myself competing with this woman because I wanted to prove my family name right. When Jack came out the house, I felt like I had won the race and made my family proud. I even called them to celebrate my success.

Afterwards, I asked Jack if he was still serious about marriage. He responded yes. I then told him that we would have to marry soon, since I had permanent change of station orders to Kirtland Air Force Base in Albuquerque, NM. We both agreed we would marry as soon as possible. We then went to his apartment to grab his belongings. While Jack was preparing to leave, he told me that my cousin did not help him pay the rent for a couple of months. Of course, I believed him again and helped him pay his bills. Pretty much I believed everything he said. Jack was one of those guys who appeared really quiet and seemed like a very nice young gentlemen. You would think that he was a priest if you did not know him. So whatever he needed me to do, I would do. I could never tell when Jack was lying because he was so smooth with it.

I was so overwhelmed by the fact of being married; I could not see any of the warning signs. The only thing I knew about Jack was what my relatives told me. They said he was a nice young man and was very reliable. Instead of seeking God's advice, I was seeking counsel from ungodly family members. Psalm 1:1 says,

> *Blessed is the man that walketh not in the counsel of the ungodly, nor standeth in the way of sinners, nor sitteth in the seat of the scornful. But his delight is in the law of the LORD; and in his law doth he meditate day and night.*

At the time, I stood in the counsel of the ungodly. These were people who had no relationship with God. I took the advice that was given to me by my cousins and made a quick decision to get married. It would have been great if I had the gift of discernment or the knowledge to ask God for His perfect will; but at that time, I did not have any knowledge of the gifts of the spirit. I barely knew the Word of God. Therefore, I continued on as planned.

We finally finished packing all of his belongings, and we were on our way to Albuquerque, New Mexico. Here we are as two strangers traveling together down I40W. I did not ask any questions; I never really got the opportunity to know him and soon we would be married. I was on my way to a sudden rude-awakening.

3

THROUGH THE VALLEY

Here we (Jack, my daughter and I) are in Albuquerque, New Mexico, the furthest Midwest I had ever been. We traveled past mountains, deserts, cactus and coyotes. There was no grass, so the scenery was dusty and everything that should have been green was brown. Finally, we made it to our destination and checked into our hotel. We still had not gotten married at this point; however, in a couple of weeks we would be. I asked God to give me a sign and let me know if he was the one. I thought because he read his Bible and he talked about the Lord he was definitely the one. I was at a point in my life where I was establishing a relationship with God. When I saw Jack reading his Bible and talking about the Lord, I thought that the Lord sent Jack into my life to bring me closer to Him. All of my choices were based off of the few conversations we had and my perceptions. Jack spent days talking about his pastor and how he was taking leadership classes at his church. Although his lips were saying one thing, I found out later that his heart was saying something totally different. From the moment we said "I do", all hell broke loose in our marriage. I recognize now that I did not marry him because I loved him. I married him because I thought he was the one for me, and I desired to be married. Overall, I should have waited and observed Jack's life long enough to see if the fruit in his life would *remain or drain.*

Today, there are a lot of women and some men who are caught up in this trap. We get caught up in believing the person is saved, but we do not wait long enough to see if the person's talk line up with his or her walk with Christ. Quite a few people shared with me that they married their spouses based on one sole purpose: the person said they were saved. Ladies and gentlemen this statement alone is not good enough.

In most marriages, there is confusion. They were confused because they took the person's word of being saved and assumed they were evenly yoked. Now they are suffering today because of their bad decisions. We have to look at the person's lifestyle and make sure that his or her life lines up with the Word of God. You cannot have Christ in your life without evidence. At some point in time, Christ should show up in their life. If there is no evidence of Christ in their lives, there should be no marriage until Christ shows up on the scene. Period.

I made an assumption that Jack was the right person. Even my best friend assumed Jack was a good Christian man. Cindy made this determination based on him reading and carrying around a Bible all the time. My mother reminded me that Jack use to always read Bible stories to my nephews. I even remembered a time when Jack and I had visited a church, and he had volunteered to pray. After the prayer service, there were a lot of women saying, "Girl, he sure can pray. She got her a good man: A praying man at that." From his outer appearance, Jack seemed like a Christian man, who loved the Lord. I used this limited information to base my choice for marriage.

I lacked direction. I did not receive any spiritual counseling. Even if I had some spiritual counseling, I am not sure I would have listened. I was on a mission to get married no matter what! There I stood at the court house saying "I do" to a man I did not know. Then all of a sudden, it all turned into a nightmare. Jack and I never became one in the spirit. We were married, but separated. In the natural, we had a marriage license, which confirmed our marriage. In the spirit realm, the marriage never took place. It was a marriage without God's blessing.

Hell Begins

Our first argument was over him getting a job. He decided that he did not want to work unless he had a job as an electrician making the same amount of money he made in Austin, TX. The cost of living in Albuquerque was less than Austin; therefore in most cases, the same job in Albuquerque would pay less than Austin. Yet, he made it clear he did not want to work unless he found a job as an electrician, paying the same or higher than what he made at his previous job. Interesting enough, he hardly looked for a job. Listen. I was disturbed and upset, on the verge of pulling my hairs out of my head. I sat there and said, "Lord I just got married to a man who I thought was going to help me and support the family. Now, he is not going to work unless he finds a specific job! You better get him because I'm about to kill him!" It was obvious my reactions to his behavior did not demonstrate the love of God. At least he could have found a job until God blessed him with the job he was looking for. Well, that was not the case. Here I am now supporting my daughter and a husband who refuses to work. To make matters worse, this behavior went on for several months.

Talking to him was like talking to a wall. It did not matter how hard life was or how much food was in the house. Jack was content watching me struggle, while he waited for the perfect job. Most of my energy was spent fussing and nagging him to get a job. No matter how much I cried or how hard I begged him to get a job, it never worked. Though he would not leave the house, he was adamant about getting a job as an electrician. I was so upset with Jack. I wanted him out of the house. I would curse the living daylights out of him and called him every word under the sun. It did not matter what I said; Jack had made up his mind. He was not going to work until he got the job he wanted.

During all of this, my daughter, Brenda, was very quiet. All along she did not agree with the decision for me to marry him. She even tried to warn me, but I did not listen. My daughter was awesome at picking up on things others could not see. Unfortunately, I did not listen to my twelve year old daughter. Everything she said about him was true. She did not believe Jack married me with the right motives. She felt like he was attractive to me physically, but there was no spiritual or emotional connection. Likewise, I married Jack for the wrong reasons. Therefore, we were both at fault. As a result of my decisions, I endured long suffering.

There were times I blamed myself for making the wrong decision to marry Jack. I looked back at the advice I received from my family, and I was mad at them. I was mad at the whole world. I was even mad at God. I wondered why He put me in this predicament. All along I believe God was saying, "Do not blame me; I did not have anything to do with that. I tried to get your attention, but you did not listen to Me. I sent people your way, but you ignore them too." When you are not spiritually mature, it is hard to be confident in hearing God's voice.

I Need Refuge

It was obvious I needed some direction and help in my situation. One of my friends got married, and she invited me to her wedding. After the wedding, I had the pleasure to meet her pastor. He had such a kind-hearted fatherly spirit. As I was leaving the church, he invited me back to the church and asked me to bring my family. I took his invitation, and that next Sunday my family and I were sitting on the front pew. I was so grateful that after looking around for a church, we finally found home. For 3 years this was my church home. What began at Cornerstone Church in San Antonio, TX continued in Albuquerque, NM.

Because of all the struggles I was facing early in my marriage, it was wonderful to have a church home with a loving pastor where I could spiritually grow. As I look back now, I realize it was the Word that kept me from falling in the pits and committing suicide. The Word is all I had. Really, that is all we need, one word from God. I had no friends. All I had was

God. I learned quickly to trust God and hold on to Him for my life support.

The Going Gets Tough

Hooray! Finally, Jack received his first job. I just knew that everything was going to go well. He found a job as an electrician, exactly what he was looking for. This job paid him more than the job in Austin, TX. I was amazed. This was unheard of and definitely a blessing from the Lord. Thank you Jesus! I finally got a husband to support me...not!

After he got his first job, he did not support us at all. By now, I was really fuming! All this time I had been waiting for Jack to get a job to help support the family, and he decided not to help support us at all! Now it was easy to see how selfish Jack was. He never paid bills unless I begged him to pay them. Since I was in the military and living on base, the housing allowance was automatically deducted from my paycheck. The only thing he was required to pay was the utility bills, but that was yet too much for him to do. Every time he got paid, I had to beg him to give me the money to pay bills. Asking him for money was like pulling teeth. He would get angry every time I would ask. I supposed he got use to me paying bills while he was unemployed for several months.

Though he was able to help with the bills financially, instead one day he brought over $200 worth of alcohol home. This was a shocker because I did not know he drank that type of liquor! All I could think was, we have bills to pay, and he's buying alcohol! I thought this alcohol thing was new, but I found out later that Jack was an alcoholic before we got married. Once again, I found out new information about the man I married. Outside of Jack buying alcohol and going to the bars, in 5 years, the only thing he bought for the house was a used lawn mower. Yep. That is it!

I was so fed up. I began to contemplate hurting Jack. One day I just snapped, and I charged him with a garden tool. Fortunately, I missed him by a long shot. Allowing my anger to get the best of me, I could have done something that would have cost me so much: my family, my career, and my life. I was hurting on the inside, and I did not know how to handle my problems. Most of the time, I would initiate the fight. We were in the ring every night. I was completely miserable, and I felt my life falling apart. I began experiencing signs of suicide. All of the pressures of home, work, and life became so unbearable.

For Worse or Worst

Jack became friends with people who would frequent bars all of the time. There would be times when he would come home after midnight. After a while, he would stop coming home at all. I would contact him, but I could never get him to answer the phone. Even one of his friends told him that he needed to call home. It was like Jack never abandoned his single life. After a while, I became suspicious of Jack cheating on me with another woman. Though I never caught him, there were obvious signs. I would find phone numbers of different women in his cell phone. There was one number he would call at least once or twice a day. One day, I dialed the number. The woman answered the phone, and I explained who I was and confronted her about her relationship with Jack. She told me that on occasion Jack would come to her house to only get his hair cut. I knew this wasn't true. Jack would always cut his own hair. He never went to a barber to get his hair cut.

While staying with his friend, Jack also admitted that he had a woman in his bedroom with no clothes on. He then explained that he did not touch her. Though I never caught Jack "in the act", I still believe that he cheated several times. However, I still was willing to make the marriage work.

Making it Work

One Sunday, my pastor preached a message that touched me. He said, "God is not going to look at the other person and ask what they did to make the marriage work. He's going to ask you!" You should have seen me. My mouth dropped! There were no more pointing fingers. God was looking at me. This message gave me strength, and I tried to make the marriage work. Gary Chapman stated in his book "The Marriage You've Always Wanted"[1], we should begin looking at the fault in ourselves before we look at the fault in our spouse. He quoted from Matthew 7:1-5 and substituted "partner" for the word "brother" so that we may see the principle at work in marriage. The scripture reads:

> Do not judge, or you too will be judged. For in the same way you judge others, you will be judged...Why do you look at the speck of sawdust in your partner's eye and pay no attention to the plank in your own eye? How can you say to your partner, "Let me take the speck out of your eye," when all the time there is a plank in your own eye? You hypocrite, first take the plank out of your own eye, and then you will

see clearly to remove the speck from your partner's eye.

Chapman goes on to say, "...that if one tries to improve her marriage by getting her husband to change (working hard to get the speck out of his eye), energies are being expended in the wrong direction. The place to begin is with one's own failures (the plank or beam in one's own eye)." I was trying to take the speck out of my husband's eye, not realizing I had a plank in my own eye. Although he did a lot of things that were unacceptable, his actions did not exempt me from doing the will of God. I was challenged to look inwardly and search my own heart. Once I began to assess my own faults, I realized there were a lot of things I was not doing. My plank prevented me from walking after the Spirit, and I was unable to see clearly. I realized that I had not applied the Word of God in my marriage or in my life.

For instance, James 5:15 says, "And the prayer of faith shall save the sick, and the Lord shall raise him up; and if he committed sins, they shall be forgiven him." I definitely did not pray for my husband's salvation nor did I pray for God to save my marriage. Unfortunately, I did not take advantage of what had been freely given to me (the power or prayer). Instead, I spent the majority of my time complaining and expecting God to perform a miracle in my marriage. I was asking God to do something He could not do: Go against His own Word and restore my marriage or my life. I had to make a choice to become a doer and not just a hearer of the Word (James 1:22). I was deceiving myself thinking that God was going to take care of everything. What I did not know was God requires us to take action. I had to stop complaining and begin praying. Even though it took every muscle in my body to love, I had to love him no matter what. Not only that, I had to "...pray for him who despitefully used me, and persecuted me" (Matthew 5:44, added emphasis). I do not care how godly you are; it takes the love of God to help you pray for your enemies.

This was all new for me. Understanding how to forgive someone was not easy. It was all a learning process. Up to this point, I just went to church and heard the Word. That was the easy part. The hard part was walking out what I just heard. This caused me to read the Bible more and find out what God's Word required me to do as a wife. Applying the Word of God is the first step in making your marriage work. Without the Word, there is no hope. Feeling sorry for yourself, complaining about your spouse, and crying is not going to change your situation. The change begins with your obedience to obey and do the Word of God.

4

CHANGE BEGINS WITH YOU

When I started changing, I wanted my husband to change too. So I started trying to change him. I thought I could change my husband by whipping him with the Word of God. Unfortunately, that did not work. I was fighting a losing battle. It was like beating a dead horse. He was spiritually dead. He could not see what I saw, he could not hear what I heard, and he did not know what I knew about God. Therefore, I was wasting my time trying to change him into something I wanted him to be. The easy mistake that we all make is trying to make someone become what we want them to become without recognizing it is important for them to become what God wants him or her to become. In most cases, when we try to make a person change, the change is only evident on the outside. Outwardly, they do what you ask them to do, but inwardly their hearts are waxed cold.

Joel Osteen gave an example in his book, *Your Best Life*

Now, about "a little boy who was in church with his mother, and he had so much energy. He just could not sit still. In fact, he kept standing up on the seat. His mother said, "Son, sit down." He'd sit down for a few seconds, and then he'd get right back up. She'd gently reprimand him again. "Son, I said to sit down!" This happened several times, and then the little boy stood up and simply would not sit down. His mother took her hand, put it on his head, and pushed him down onto the seat. The boy sat there smiling. Finally, he looked at his mother and said, "Mom, I may be sitting down on the outside, but I'm standing on the inside" (Osteen, 187,188)!

This story reminds me of the time when I tried to make my husband stop smoking. He would tell me over and over again that he had stopped smoking, but I would always catch him smoking cigarettes. With his mouth he would tell me he changed, but in his heart he remained the same (Matthew 15:8).

The best and only solution I have found is to pray that God would change a person's heart. The only One who has the ability to change a person's heart is the Lord. However, the person must first have a desire to change. Trying to change someone who does not want to change will only create frustration, headaches, and pain in your life. We must recognize that the change begins with you.

Most of the time we look at the things our spouses are lacking in a relationship. Seldom, do we look at ourselves. We fail to look within and see what we are not doing or what can we do better to make our marriage succeed. You can go on and on trying to change your spouse, but it is never going to work.

My experience is a prime example. Through the process, I learned that the one person we can change is ourselves. The first change is to start obeying the Word of God and praying for your spouse's salvation. Once God sets the person free, he is truly free because whoever the Son sets free is free indeed (John 8:36). As long as you are doing your part, God will do His part. My part was to pray and wait on God. If my marriage was meant to be, it will be. For whatever marriages God has joined, there is no man who can separate them. That includes you and me. I believe that if the marriage is not ordained by God and not in His perfect will, then God will either supernaturally change the person's life to line up with His will or that person will be removed. Until then, remain faithful to your marriage vows, "For better or worse, for richer or poorer, so help me God."

Here Comes Baby

One day, totally out of the blue, my husband said he wanted a divorce because I did not want to have a child. He knew exactly how I felt about having children because before we got married we agreed to not have any children. Now, almost two years after being married, he told me he wants to have a child or else he wants a divorce.

Making a decision to have a child was a tough decision. We were already having problems in the marriage, so why bring a child into all this chaos? I pondered on the thought for several days and decided to have a child. I thought that this would resolve some of our issues. Unfortunately, after I got pregnant, our marriage had gone from worse to worst. Jack left the house more than ever. I was deceived again. We were back where we started. The only difference, I was pregnant and frustrated. Going to church on Sunday was one of my most embarrassing moments. There I was pregnant and with no husband. How would I explain Jack's absence from the family? He had chosen the bars and friends over the family and church. Going to church alone and being pregnant was one of the hardest obstacles to overcome. I was constantly wondering what people thought about me. I felt like an outcast. This was definitely a difficult time in my life, but God helped me through it. The Word of God was the only thing that kept me alive. God was my life support. I was barely hanging on to my last breath, and I could not afford to be disconnected from my Source.

Finally, the day came. I gave birth to a beautiful 6 lb and 2oz little girl, Candace. After the delivery, there was a complete shift in our marriage. I thought having a child would take away the pain and make our marriage better. Not at all! During my delivery, I had some difficulties. My daughter's heart rate kept decreasing extremely low. The doctor had to rush and do an emergency C-section. Anyone who has ever had a C-section understands the pain and stress it is on one's body. Normally, the doctor directs you to take it easy and stay off your feet for 6 weeks until your body recovers and heals. Putting too much stress on the body would cause excessive bleeding and lead you back to the hospital. I thought that Jack would take the load off and help out while I recovered. Instead, he spent most of his time playing video games or visiting his friends. At the time, because of my decision to have a child, I was torn apart. All I could do was just curl up in a ball and cry out to the Lord. I cried so hard that both of my eyes were swollen shut. It looked like I had just come out of a boxing match. When

I made a decision to have a child, I thought I was making the right decision. I realized later that I should have waited until things had gotten better.

Facing problems in my marriage was not the only thing I was going through. I was battling with recovering from the C-section and my newborn faced many medical challenges. She had difficulties breathing, and since she was so young, there was not too much the doctors could do. It seemed like every day, we were taking her back and forth to the hospital. Trying to get Jack to help was a losing battle. Within a couple of days, I was up and running. I had no choice. I even drove to the store several times to pick up some items for the little one, while my constant prayer was "Lord, please do not allow me to go back to the hospital." My condition was beyond stress. If you would have pushed me another inch, I would have fallen over the cliff. I was that far gone. All of what was going on in my life is what took me to another level of trust and faith in God.

There was no man who could supply my need. No matter what people would say, my problems still existed. I went to bed at night and woke up with the same problem. That's how I learned to trust God. I understand that friends and family are there when we are going through things in our lives, but they do not have the power to change your life. I was in pursuit of life. Death was already trying to take me. It even began to call my daughter's (Candace) name. Many days she fought for her very life, gasping for oxygen. Finally, the doctors hooked her up to a breathing machine. Imagine dealing with a sick child and no emotional or spiritual support from her father.

There was one time we almost lost our daughter. Somehow she stopped receiving oxygen. As she laid in my arms, her face turned blue, and I witnessed the very life departing from her little body. I was hysterical and did not know what to do. I thought, "My baby is about to die in my arms, and there is nothing I can do." Her oxygen had been completely shut off. When I began to blow into her mouth, God supernaturally restored her oxygen flow. Through all of this, Jack did not say anything. He did not move. Jack did not seem a bit concern. There was no emotional support whatsoever. Sometimes I wondered if he had any feelings or emotions towards anyone else other than himself.

Most of the time, it was my mother and I who took my daughter to the hospital. My mother understood the opposition in my marriage, so she traveled 200 miles to help us out. If it was up to my mom, she would have left Jack a long time ago. My mother really disapproved of how he treated me and the family. She knew just how miserable I was with life.

One day I was talking to one of the ladies at my church, and I expressed to her that I wanted to die and go home with the Lord. Then all my pain and hurt will be gone. Why should I live? I have a daughter who is sick, and each day I do not know if she would live to see another day. On top of that, I have a husband who is barely at home and does not provide any support. The easy way out, I thought, was to die and go home to be with Jesus. That's just how bad it was for me. I regretted the day I was born and the day I brought a child into my terrible situation. My life had completely turned for the worse while I was going through all of these physical, spiritual, mental, and emotional battles.

As I mentioned earlier, Jack spent most of his time playing

video games than he did supporting the family. Sometimes he would stay locked up in the room for hours playing different games. What made it even worse is that Jack found other men in the church who had the same addiction. I thought someone would lead Jack in the right direction and encourage him to support his family. Well, that didn't happen. No one counseled him on how important it would be to support his family during all of the battles that were going on. They took turns going over to each other's houses several days during the week playing video games. There were times it would be really late at night, and Jack would not call home and check on the family. I would try calling him to see when he would get home. Believe it or not, his friends and their wives treated me disrespectfully when I called. Sometimes they would lie and say he was not there. Now, these are supposedly my Christian brothers and sisters. You talk about support; there was not any at all! The only support I had was the Lord. That's why I held so close to Him.

How do you deal with this kind of behavior? What do you do next when you've done all you can? At least I thought I did all I could do. I did everything in my own strength. My cup had ran out, and I did not have any more energy.

My Cup Runneth Out

Everyday it was another battle. If it was not one thing, then it was another. So guess what? You got it! We were back where we had started. He was laid off from his job, and he did not want to get another job unless it was the type of job he wanted or paid a certain amount of money. Now, we are living off of one income again. We have a new addition to the family, so now I'm providing for a family of four and two dogs. I went from riches to rags very quickly. Before I got married, I never had any financial difficulties. My oldest daughter and I could go out and eat as much as we wanted. Now, I was in a position where I could barely put food on the table. This was a road I had never traveled. I thought having a child would change Jack's perspective. The only thing that changed was the number of dependents I was taking care of. He did not want to do simple things such as cut the grass, clean the house, or take out the trash even though he was home all day. It did not matter if the baby had food or not. Jack still would not get a job or help support the family in any way. He was very selfish and only took care of himself. If it was something that benefited him, he would be all over it. Other than that, you could forget it.

Having a child did not make a difference. For someone who said he wanted a child, he really had a great way of expressing his love and affection. Before he got laid off from his job, I had to practically beg him to buy diapers and food for his daughter. To put it all in a nut shell, I married a man who did not want to work and certainly did not want to support the family, emotionally, physically, financially or spiritually.

I was paying for two vehicles, which were both Sport Utility Vehicles (SUVs). I kept both vehicles because Jack promised that he would get another job and make the payments. Time went on and Jack still did not get a job. By then, payments were terribly draining me and everything in my bank account. To pay for the vehicles were already a challenge, but to keep gas in them was another chore. Every three days, I would fill my tank again. With the new baby, we had incurred $400 childcare expenses as well as buying all the baby supplies and food while taking care of my oldest daughter in high school. I became so stressed and discouraged with all the bills that one day I began to wail on the side of the road uncontrollably in my vehicle, asking the Lord to help me. Through my sincere tears, I heard the voice of the Lord speak so clearly and say, "Sell both of your SUVs and get a more economical vehicle." There were other changes I made to provide more for the family. Within four weeks, I sold both of my vehicles. I turned the cable off, disconnected my oldest daughter's cell phone, and changed our home phone to the basic service. When it was all said and done, all of my savings accounts were empty and bank account drained. In the midst of all of this happening, Jack responded: "You made me suffer; now I'm going to watch you suffer." Jack blamed me for taking him away from his single life.

My cup ran out! *But* when I look back, I know that obeying the Lord and making adjustments made it possible for us to live. There were times after making adjustments to our finances that I thought Jack was changing for the better. All I could think was finally, he was ready to take care of his responsibilities and step in his role as head of the household. Jack convinced me that if he got a van to perform a particular job he would help support the family. Unfortunately, I was deceived again. One thing Jack was good at was telling lies. If lies were an occupation, he would qualify as the best in the business.

There was another time when Jack appeared very excited about getting a job at the fire department. Of course, I was thrilled about his eagerness to get a job, so he could finally support the family. In order to get a job with the fire department, Jack had to successfully pass a physical training and a written test. I knew how important it was for him to study, so I decided to take the kids 200 miles away to their grandmother's house, so he could study and have some peace in the house. Only to my surprise I had been deceived again. I found out later that Jack did not study at all. While I was gone, he did other things and blew the test off.

In this time, my love increased for God. If it was not for the Lord, I would not be here today. My marriage was tearing my life and family apart. We were dying spiritually, emotionally, financially and physically. I had hit rock bottom, laying flat on my face.

Is There Still Hope

Nothing seemed to change. I wanted Jack gone. I did not care if it was out the house or out of this world. I wanted him completely out of my life. I had problems at home and at work. At work, I had a boss who did not like me because of his racial issues with multiculturalism in the military. I had all this going on at work, and I was living in hell at home. Everyday was difficult. Suicide was not far from my mind. I entertained the thought numerous times, just never carried it out. I thought about divorce, but this scripture kept me encouraged:

> And if a woman has a husband who is not a believer and he is willing to live with her, she must not divorce him. For the unbelieving husband has been sanctified through his wife." (1 Corinthians 7:13-14, NIV)

Then I thought about what the church would say if they saw me with two children and no husband. What do I do? Lord, "Can I leave?" Must I continue with this emotional, mental, spiritual, financial, and physical abuse?" Would you hate me if I divorced? What are my options? I had crazy thoughts like, "I guess the only way out of this marriage is to kill myself or to kill him!" Of course, we know that is not the answer. I cried to the Lord: "I need direction. I cannot handle this abuse in my own strength. I need a word…something from You, Lord".

What I experienced at this point in my marriage was worth me waiting on the Lord for my mate. God did not ordain for me to suffer like this. God says in Jeremiah 29:11, "For I know the thoughts that I think toward you, saith the Lord, thoughts of peace, and not of evil, to give you an expected end." I had to constantly remind myself of the hope that God had given me through His Word. Though many days, it seemed like all hope was gone. "Hope deferred makes the heart sick" (Proverbs 13:12). I did not want to live my life with a sick heart.

Several times my mother would say she could not see how I was still standing. She said it was the Lord who saved me. I know it was. *But* I found Him to be my Strong Tower in a time of great need.

The name of the Lord is a strong tower: the righteous Runneth into it, and is safe. (Proverbs 18:10)

I fell in His arms and trusted Him each day for directions. I thought I had no more to give, but God showed me what could and would happen when I began to trust Him in a greater way.

5
TURNED OVER

I had a lot of questions and no answers. While all this was going on in my life, I had changed jobs. Whenever you change jobs in the military, we have to receive technical training for the new occupation. My training was held in Cocoa Beach, Florida. I was scheduled for a temporary duty assignment (TDY) for four months. That meant Jack would have to take care of the children while I was gone.

In the past, he had never proven himself to take care of the children. I feared something would happen before I returned from my training, so I called my mother and asked would she stay with the family until I returned from TDY. After all I had gone through, I did not trust the kids with him alone. Especially since my youngest daughter needed medical attention. My mother understood the situation; so without hesitation, she drove up again. A couple of days after she arrived, I was headed to Florida on the plane. I had no idea that my trip to

Florida would completely change my life. For four months, it seemed as I was swallowed up in the belly of a fish. When the Lord brought me ashore from my training, I was a new person.

Not long after I arrived in Florida, I started losing my eyesight. Prior to then, I had 20/20 vision. Overnight, my vision had tremendously decreased. My vision had gotten so weak, I had one of my classmates take me to the Ophthalmologist. When the diagnosis came back, the doctor told me that I was border line for driving, and I needed eyeglasses. The doctor could not determine why the sudden change in my eyesight. They did blood work, but still could not find anything. Ladies and Gentlemen, it seemed like all odds were against me. To this day, my mother believed it was the emotional and mental stress in my marriage that caused my eyesight to decrease drastically. After seeing the ophthalmologist, I got new glasses.

Though many things were happening in my life, there was hope. My oldest sister, whom I mentioned earlier, told her father that I was in Florida. When he heard I was in Florida, he wanted to visit me. From now on, I will reference him as my father.

It was close to the end of my assignment when my father and I finally met again. His wife and youngest son drove up to Cocoa Beach. Since I was staying in a suite, they all stayed with me. It was really hard for both us to say anything. He understood the soreness, hurt, and unforgiveness I carried in my heart for many years after he and my mom divorced. So, he began to share with me what happened 20 some years ago and why things went the way they did. Afterwards, I forgave my father, and I asked if he would forgive me. Of course, he said yes.

God had restored our relationship. That very moment I felt a weight come off of me. I was released from the pain and anger I once held for over 20 years. We were able to leave the past behind us and fully embrace our future. To this day, we have an awesome relationship. Reuniting me with my father was not the only thing God had in store for me. It was just the beginning, and the best was yet to come!

One Night With The King

The day before my departure was a day I will never forget. As I completed my last day of training and departed my class, I was approached by two military individuals (one officer and one enlisted personnel). They asked me if I would join them at an upscale club. My first response was "No!" My answer turned out to be not good enough for them. They kept insisting that I go. Finally, I told them that I was a Christian, and I did not feel right going to the club. They looked at me like I had completely lost my mind and ostracized me for my decision. I had to choose life or death. I understood death, and knew I did not like it. Though it would have been easy to go to a club where no one would have ever known, I decided to choose life over the death they were presenting me. So far, death is all that I had experienced in my marriage, and I did not want to choose that route again.

Later that same day, I got my hair done, and it looked great! When the hairdresser had finished styling my hair, I thought I was the best looking thing since slice bread. As I looked in the mirror at my hair, the voice of the enemy said, "You know you look good. You need to go to the club." The voice became louder and louder. Finally, I told myself I was not going. Instead, I decided to visit a church I had been attending while I was in Florida. On Sunday, they had announced that they would be selling books that the pastor and another woman had written. I decided to go to the church and pick up a copy before I left for home.

This was definitely a move by God because I did not travel during the night. When my vision decreased, it was really difficult for me to see at night. For some reason, this time, it did not matter. I was determined to receive a copy of the book before returning home. I pulled into the church's parking lot excited about receiving my book. As I walked through the doubled-glass doors into the sanctuary, I ran into the woman who co-authored the book. When I approached her, she looked me in my eyes and said, "I do not normally give these books out. Normally someone else gives them out for us, but there is a reason why you are here, and I'm talking to you." At that moment, I could tell that she had a keen sense of discernment. Though I did not understand exactly what she was talking about, I knew I had to listen.

She sat down in a room at the back of the church, and she began to speak words into my life. The Lord spoke through her and revealed personal things about my life. She said, "God hears your cry, and He sees your tears as they drain on your pillow." At that moment, I began to weep. During that entire week, I had been crying out to the Lord with tears streaming from my face to the pillow every night. I questioned the Lord about my marriage and why I had to suffer so much. I also questioned about my life, and even got to the point of asking if He was really real. I wanted to know why I had so much confusion in my life. This woman shared everything about my life.

You would think this woman lived in my bedroom. Before this point, I had never met God in this way.

On that day, God became more real to me than He ever had. I had never seen anyone operate prophetically as she did. She told me that when she prayed for me, I would be totally out of it for at least 30 minutes (slain in the spirit as many may call it). I thought this woman had lost her mind; yet, I went alone with her. While she was praying, I kept thinking about not being able to move when she finished. Finally, she had finished praying and I thought, "Yeah, right! I'll be able to move." My thoughts were so wrong.

After she said amen, I tried to open my eyes and get up from my seat only to find I was unable to! I could not move! I tried to move, but I could not get up at all. The only thing active was my mind. I could sense the Spirit of the Lord, and His presence and glory so heavily filled the room. I could feel His touch like never before. All I could do was cry. I could feel Him hold me in His arms and comforted me from all the pain and sufferings I had endured. As I was crying, the woman said with a calm and peaceful voice, "Jesus came here today just for you. Do not feel guilty. He has forgiven you of all your sins." She was right again. I felt guilty for doubting God as the Creator of the earth and questioned His very existence. From that day, I never doubted God again. I knew He was real, and I was standing face-to-face with Jesus. Just to know that God was on my side was enough for me. That was truly my one night with the King, and I enjoyed every moment of it.

Changed

After my moment with the King of Glory, I was finally able to get up from my seat. When I got up, I was a changed person. I felt like I was walking on water. There was a spiritual transformation in my life. The Lord had filled me with His Spirit. I had been born of water, but I had never been born of the Spirit. This was an experience I cannot explain. Jesus explains being born of the Spirit like this:

> The wind blows wherever it pleases. You hear it sound, but you cannot tell where it comes from or where it is going. So it is with everyone born of the Spirit. (John 3:8, NIV)

From that day forward, it was the Holy Spirit who helped me through all the obstacles in my marriage. I realized that before then I was doing everything in my own strength. Though I had a choice to go out to the club or church, I chose God and He was waiting for me when I arrived.

Life With The Spirit

Sometimes I sit back and wonder how many times I missed God. How many times was God waiting for me, and I never showed up? God had an appointment for me, and He reached down and lifted me out of my pit. He filled me with His Spirit, so I could endure the days to come. It was no longer I, but it was Christ in me that strengthened me to live another day and to face the obstacles not only in my marriage, but everyday life.

Once I received the Holy Spirit, I could hear the voice of

the Lord so clearly. I began having conversations with God. One of our first conversations, He said, "You never considered me in your marriage." Wow. In other words, when I was contemplating divorce I never consulted Him. I was trying to exit my marriage without God's consent. I knew it was true. I fell to my knees and asked the Lord to forgive me.

Now, God was asking me to wait on Him to direct my decisions for my marriage. My first response to God's request surely was not "Yes Lord! Send me I'll go." That was the last thing on my mind. Many times I wanted to walk out and throw in my towel. If I could have gotten away with murder, I probably would have chosen that route. I was just that desperate for an escape.

However, my experience with God really changed my life. The things I use to do, I just did not want to do them anymore. It was easy to ignore God and disobey His commands. But, now, the Holy Spirit was bringing conviction to my heart. I could not do what *I* wanted to do anymore. I had to die to selfishness (doing things my way) and live to righteousness (doing it God's way). I thought about my life and what I had to endure, and I wondered, "Why do I have to allow God to guide my footsteps? I found the answer to my question in these scriptures:

If you love me, you will obey what I command. (John 14:15, NIV)

For ye are dead, and your life is hid with Christ in God (Colossians 3:3).

This was the real test. Do I really love the Lord? Did I really die to myself and my own desires? My faith actions would now have to prove it. God promised that if I would surrender my life to Him, He would answer another question: *Will the*

Lord Save My Marriage or Save My Life or both? So I surrendered my life to Him and obeyed His voice. I did not want to make the same mistakes going out as I did coming into the marriage. I wanted to see what God would do on my behalf.

THE PROCESS

6

KEEP ON, KEEPING ON

When God told me to wait on Him, I just knew He was going to save my marriage, so I was on my best behavior, trying to do everything right according to the Word. I flew back to Albuquerque, preparing for my next assignment at Tinker Air Force Base, located in Oklahoma City, Oklahoma.

Once I arrived back to Albuquerque, a few days before I moved to Oklahoma City, the Lord opened doors for me to preach my first message. I was definitely excited. I preached from the book of Job in the Old Testament. The title of my message was "How Firm is your Foundation?" I related the life of Job to what was going on in my own life and how the enemy was trying to destroy everything in my possession. Satan took all Job's children, servants, livestock, herdsmen and home. Then he tried to attack his health. I was definitely having a Job experience. I was losing my marriage, my finances, my mind, my vehicle, and my home. Additionally, I almost lost my daughter, my health (eyesight), and my true purpose for living. Imagine losing everything you had and at the same time continuing to worship God no matter what. It is one thing to praise, but it is another thing to worship. Worship means to show the worth of something or someone. Through all of this, Job still worshipped the Lord for who He was in his life.

> *Job arose and rent his mantle and shaved his head, and fell down upon the ground, and worshipped. And said, Naked came I out of my mother's womb, and naked shall I return thither; the Lord gave, and the Lord hath take away; blessed be the name of the Lord. In all this Job sinned not, nor charged God foolishly. (Job 1:20-22)*

In spite of all his losses, Job chose to worship. He stood on a firm foundation and trusted God no matter what. It was through the message I preached that gave me more faith to stand even when it looked like hope had packed its bags and moved away. I knew that whatever was happening in my life God was fully aware and the devil had no authority to take my possessions.

The life of Job is an inspiration to me. His experiences and his love for God taught me how to wait on my blessing. At the end of Job's life, the Bible says that his latter days were greater than his beginning (Job 42:12). That was my hope. I knew that my latter days were greater than what I had gone through by this point in my life, and God had a plan of deliverance just for me.

Now I understand why the Psalmist said, "O taste and see that the Lord is good: blessed is the man that trusteth in him" (Psalm 34:8). The only way that we can see that God is good is to trust Him. I thought about this, and what I'm about to say is so true. You cannot love someone until you fully trust them. Without trust, doubt is always lingering around somewhere. I had to put my trust in God when He asked me to wait on Him. As I began to fall more and more in love with God, I found that I trusted Him so much more.

Each day God gave me peace, love and strength. It was not by happenstance that I chose to pick up that book in Florida. God knew what was before me. If it was not for the Lord standing before me, I honestly do not believe I would be here today writing my testimony.

Trusting God Even More

Before I left Florida, I promised God that I would release my marriage to Him, and that's exactly what I did. The option to divorce was no longer in my possession. When I passed the baton, I did not take it back. God was the captain of my ship; whichever way He turned I followed. He called the cadence; I responded.

The only difference was that I did not allow the things that affected me in the past to affect my future. In a bad situation, I chose to have a good day. Most of the things that bothered me in the past I did not allow them to get the best of me. My focus was on God. In the past, I would try to work things out in my marriage on my own. This time I sought out Christian counsel. I thought this would be a good start and could possibly save our marriage.

We had our first counseling session with our Bishop in Albuquerque. He did his best to lead us on the right path according to the Word of God. Of course, Jack never felt like he needed counseling. It seemed that everything went in one ear and out the other. That's okay. I still did what God called me to do.

Happiness or sadness or wealth should not keep anyone from doing God's work. (I Corinthians 7:30, NLT)

A few days after we arrived in Oklahoma City, things still were not getting better in our marriage. I wanted to retreat by throwing in the towel and saying: "Satan you win." If you gave me your towel, I would have thrown it in too. I was just that mad. Then I heard the Lord say in the midst of my frustrations, "Sabrina you are better than that. You are my child." The Lord reminded me that "I am more than a conqueror through him that loved me" (Romans 8:37, emphasis added).

I continued to seek a resolution for our marriage, so I immediately found a counselor who had doctorates in Christian counseling. While we were in the counseling session, the pastor looked Jack directly into his eyes and said, "Listen Son! You need to get a job and help your family." I knew a godly anger had come over that pastor. He was able to see straight through Jack. Before then, everyone thought Jack was so quiet and did everything just right. If you did not know him, you would think that he was an angel.

During our counseling session, the Holy Spirit revealed Jack's true fruit. The pastor could see right through his lies and knew that I was crying out for help. I continued to go through the process and followed God's direction. Out of the kindness of the Pastor's heart, he gave us some food. I never asked for a dime or anything. He just called the house one day and told us to come to the church and pick up some food. Every time it seemed like we were down to our last drop of food, the Lord would provide.

The Lord had to break me down just so I could take my eyes off "self" and place them on Him. God was trying to get my attention, but I was too stubborn to listen. My main focus was my husband and what he was doing. I did not look to God for my supply. I continued to focus on my husband, expecting him to meet my needs. I argued with him daily about getting a job and helping me pay the bills. It was so much easier telling my husband what to do rather than trusting and waiting on the Lord to work it out. I totally ignored Philippians 4:19: "God shall supply all my need according to his riches in glory by Christ Jesus."

After my one night with the King, I have learned to "Cast all my anxiety on him because he cares for me" (1 Peter 5:7, emphasis added, NIV). Because of my obedience, the Lord answered my prayers.

...your Father knows the things you have need of before you ask Him. (Matthew 6:8)

I found that God already knew my need and that is why the need was always supplied. As long as I followed God and obeyed His voice, He provided in ways I couldn't imagine. My true Source was God. I learned that our Creator is far greater than His creation, and He "...is able to do exceeding abundantly above all that we ask or think, according to the power that worketh in us" (Ephesians 3:20).

There were plenty days we barely had groceries in the house. One Christmas, we did not have any food or money. I chose not to pressure Jack to help us. Instead, I took my request unto the Lord. I prayed, "Lord I do not have any food or money. All I ask from You is some money, so I can feed my children on Christmas." Immediately, the Lord heard my cry. He placed on my father's heart to send us some money for the first time in over 20 years. That was God! Then my two sisters and my mother sent money. Tears of joy began to fall from my eyes with thanksgiving unto the Lord. I began to see God manifest Himself in my life when I started trusting in Him.

God had met my needs in so many ways. Another time, the family support center (an agency that helps military families in need) provided me with some food and a check to buy some other items. I was so grateful for their support. They really lived up to their name and provided support to my family in a desperate time of need.

When you trust God, He will definitely make a way when it seems like there is no way. God said "We shall call upon him, and he will answer us: He will be with us in trouble; he will deliver us, and honor us. With long life will he satisfy us, and show us his salvation."

In the scripture, Psalm 91, God promised that if we call upon His name, He would:

1. Answer us.

2. Be with us in trouble.

3. Deliver us.

4. Honor us.

5. Satisfy us with a long life.

6. Show us His salvation.

What a promise! Trust God and know that He hears your cry, and He promised to set the captives free. You may have entered into the wilderness by yourself, but you will not come out alone. God will set you free. Do not think for one second that God does not stand ready to pull you out of the fiery fire. Whatever need you have, it has been already met. God never intended for your needs to be met by a man or a woman.

Apostle Paul wrote to the Philippians mainly to thank them for their generous gifts. He goes on to say near the end of his letter: Listen up…I have something to tell you: "And my God will meet all your needs according to his glorious riches in Christ Jesus" (Philippians 4:19, NIV). I'm a witness. God met my needs. Jack could not meet the needs. I took them off Jack and placed them on my Jehovah-Jireh (the Lord will provide).

When you trust God, rest assured that your weeping may endure for a while, but your joy is destined to come in the morning (Psalm 30:5, emphasis added).

You Can Trust Him Too

What God is about to do in your life, we cannot even fathom. God has a greater plan for you. Your current situation is not your destiny. Trust Him to provide, restore, deliver, and heal. The more you trust in God, the easier it will be to let go. Fighting the situation is not worth it anymore. It only tears you apart. You never know how God will come through for you.

> *How do you know, wife, whether you will save your husband? Or, how do you know, husband, whether you will save your wife? (1 Corinthians 7:16)*

Be willing to die to yourself and endure the ride until God gives you an answer. Surrender your marriage to the Lord. Do not take it back from Him. Allow your trust in Him to grow stronger and watch Him work on your behalf.

7

SPEAK TO THE MOUNTAIN

Complaining has gotten people in more trouble than any-thing. I heard one minister say: "You complain when you are married, and you complain when you are not married." In the past, I would complain all the time. That's the only way I knew how to deal with my problems. I talked *about* my mountains (marital problems) to the Lord, never *to* my mountains. But once I started going through the process, I began to speak to the mountains in my life and say, "Be thou removed in the name of Jesus." Whatever I needed God to remove (a bad marriage, sickness, disease, anger, etc), I spoke to the situation and cast it down. As long as I complained about my problems, it had dominion over me. When I spoke to my problems, I took dominion over them and the enemy's devices. The tricks the enemy used in the past no longer worked. His tricks only became operative when I gave more attention to the problem (enemy) than the solution (God).

Disobedience kept me bound and from receiving the promises of God for my life. The same happened with Moses when he disobeyed God's specific instructions (Read Numbers 20:7-12). The Lord commanded Moses to speak to the rock to bring forth water. Instead, Moses lifted up his rod and struck the rock twice. He disobeyed God, and his disobedience kept him from entering into the promise land (Read Deuteronomy 32:48-52).

If I had continued to choose disobedience as a way of life, I would have missed out on my blessing and never entered into God's promises for my life. Any obstacle that came up against me or my family, I spoke to them with faith filled words and got rid of them. Start "calling those things which be not as though they were" (Romans 4:17, emphasis added). Though the situation looks bad, speak words of life to it. Begin to say things like, "My marriage is prosperous, and it shall live and not die in the name of Jesus." Some days it may look like nothing is happening as you confess and believe, but if you wait patiently you will definitely see results. When I saw depression leave and frustrations disappear, I knew I could begin to live a life of freedom in the midst of the troubles. Release your problems to the Lord, and you will be released from condemnation.

Usually, it is not the mountain that trips us up; it is the small obstacles that are overlooked along the way. When I ignored the small things in my marriage, they elevated and soon formed mountains. The sooner you take authority and speak to the situations that arise in your life, the quicker you will walk in freedom. God made us the "Head" and not the tail. The devil is beneath our feet. God gives us the authority and the power through the Holy Spirit to make changes in our lives.

From the beginning, we were created to speak and see change. It began in Genesis 2:18, when God gave Adam authority to name every animal. Whatever he called it, so it was. Now think about how walking in that authority can bless your own life. It is up to us to walk in obedience to His Word and decide what we will call our marriages...our lives: life or death is in your mouth.

Crucify the Flesh

Therefore if any man be in Christ, he is a new creature: old things are passed away; **behold,** *all things are become new. (II Corinthians 5:17)*

So the process continues. God challenged me to check myself. I began to check all areas of my own life to make sure that there was nothing I was doing to hinder my marriage from prospering. Not only was I challenged to watch my mouth, but now I was challenged everyday to walk in the new man that God created me to be. I did not know if God was going to save my marriage; however, I pressed on as if He would. I filled my mouth with praise to Him. Some days were harder than others. Many times I had to bite my tongue from complaining, but I knew that crucifying my flesh was the only way that I could put a stop to the enemy. Truthfully, the devil is really not after your marriage. He's after your life. As long as I gave way to the enemy, he got closer to taking me out.

Early in my marriage, I continued to operate in the flesh (cursing, fussing, and yelling). As a result, I allowed the enemy to control my words, my marriage, and my life. Although, Ephesians 4:27 told me to, "Neither give place to the devil", I did it anyway...with my mouth. Though I knew what the

Word of God said to do, I did not operate in the fruit of the Spirit according to Galatians 5:22-23, which says, "But the fruit of the Spirit is love, joy, peace, longsuffering, gentleness, goodness, faith, meekness, temperance: against such there is no law."

I questioned: Since my husband did not walk after the Spirit, why should I walk after the Spirit? Besides, I did not want to waste my time on someone who did not care about me. Therefore, out of selfishness, I refused to walk in love. I did not allow the peace of God to dwell in my heart, and I had no desire to long suffer and wait on the Lord for my husband to change.

Because I refused to walk after the Spirit, works of the flesh manifested: Adultery, fornication, uncleanness, lasciviousness, idolatry, witchcraft, hatred, variance, emulations, wrath, strife, seditions, heresies, envyings, murders, drunkenness, reveling, and such like" (Galatians 5:19-21). Yes, the works (hatred, strife, & wrath) of the flesh were absolutely on their J-O-B in my marriage. For God to restore my marriage, I had to grow up and stop acting like a child. I had to put an end to repaying evil for evil. Just because he hung out all night did not make it right for me to hang out all night. Just because he went to the bars did not give me permission to hang out at the bars. Apostle Paul says it like this:

> *When I was a child, I spake as a child, I understood as a child, I thought as a child: but when I became a man, I put away childish things. (I Corinthians 13:11)*

As I began to mature in the Word, I had to put away childish things and stop allowing my husband's negative conduct to effect my walk with Christ. When I crucified my flesh, I started speaking kind words to my husband even when he was being rude and ugly towards me. I had to stop telling him to get a job and start praying that he would find a job. I had to do a "180 degree" turn.

Changing was not an easy process. Sometimes it was painful. Later I found out that obeying the Word may hurt, but the same Word that hurts is the same Word that came back around and healed the deep wounds. I began to see drastic change in my life. Depression left my body. I stopped having ulcers. I learned to *"accept the things I could not change…walk in the courage to change the things I could and have the wisdom to know the difference"* (emphasis added).

Overall, my mind, soul, body and spirit were rejuvenated. Allowing God to lead you will relieve a lot of unnecessary stress in your life and give you the strength to face another day. Trust that God will see you through. Know that He will soon reveal His true purpose for your marriage.

Let Go and Let God

As we go through the process, our faith is often tested. Out of frustration and disappointment, I wanted to pack my husband's luggage, put him in them and send him far away. I wanted to literally kick him out the house. But every time I tried to put him out, God said "No!" Though I submitted, it hurt so much to obey God's voice. I was like a child kicking and screaming, trying to get God to change His mind. Of course, that did not work. I had to let go and let God. The only strength I had was to sit still:

For the Egyptians shall help in vain, and to no purpose: therefore, - "have I cried concerning this," - their strength is to sit still. (Isaiah 30:7)

I needed to go somewhere and sit down! As a child, my grandmother use to tell us to go somewhere and sit down. We did not argue with Big Mama because we knew what was coming next if we did not listen. My grandmother would lay a switch on our rear end! The same fear I had for my grandmother I had even more for God. So when God told me to sit down, I sat my hind down.

Do not become a fixer. Step out of God's way. Let it go. To let go means to let go of your pride, your anger, your unforgiveness, your hurt and your pain. You have to let go everything that's standing between the promise and the performance of the promise. "...lay aside every weight, and sin which doth so easily beset us, and let us run with patience the race that is set before us" (Hebrew 12:1). Sometimes it is hard to let go of things you have held onto for so long. It is like nurturing a newborn baby. When the baby cries, you pick it up. When the baby is hungry, you feed it. For the most part, you carry the responsibility. Eventually, babies grow up, and we have to let them go. Although it may be hard for some of us to let go, we have to let go.

The same goes for our marriages. We have to let go and let God do the nurturing and the feeding. As long as we continue to pick up our marriages like babies to feed and nurture it, God cannot begin to restore. He cannot fix something that we have our hands on.

I know it is hard to let go and to do the right thing. Do not think for one minute I do not understand. I'm writing to you something I've lived, not some good story I heard about. I experienced the pain and the hurt. God did not intervene until I finally took my hands off of my marriage once and for all. I had to release all of that weight (anger, pain, frustration, and controlling spirits) and stop fighting against God rather than fighting with Him.

I believe we have a problem with letting go of things for several reasons. One, we do not trust and believe that God will work it out. Two, we are not ready to hear God's answer, or lastly, we do not have the patience to wait on Him. When God does not work in the realm of our time tables, we feel God is taking too long, so we then take matters into our own hands. I would always try to work out my own problems, not realizing I was digging my own grave.

I believe it is God's desire to see us released from the hindrances of life. He is calling out to His sons and daughters saying:

Come unto me, all ye that labour and are heavy laden, and I will give you rest. Take my yoke upon you, and learn of me; for I am meek and lowly in heart: and ye shall find rest unto your souls. For my yoke is easy, and my burden is light. (Matthew 11:28 -30).

Release your burdens to the Lord. Lay your problems and concerns at the feet of Jesus.

My heart cries, shouts, and calls out to you in the wilderness. Do not allow Satan to get the best of you and destroy your true purpose for living. Let go of everything right now. Lay it down at the cross and allow Jesus to wipe your tears and lead you in the right direction. I promise if you heed the voice of the Lord, He will definitely guide you in making the right decision in your marriage and life.

Remember, your life is worth living. God wants you to live and so do I.

8

PORN...BE GONE

Just when I was moving victoriously for several months in trusting God and believing Him to work things out for my good, I was slapped with another surprise. Apparently, Jack had an addiction to pornography that I did not know anything about. After dealing with the lies, bars, clubs, video games, the pornography put the icing on the cake.

First of all, his actions were a disgrace to the marriage and my family. Jack always had an excuse for his actions. His excuse for indulging in pornography was because we were not having sex. This was true when we first got married, but during this time, that was not the case. Unfortunately, the pornography was bigger in Jack's life than I thought. In these times, I realized that when I said "I do", I said "I do" to the whole package: pornography, lies, selfishness, and all!

All of sudden, it seem like pornography was everywhere. Every time I turned around there was pornography. It was in the garage, under the bed mattress and in his vehicle. It was really out of control. He had all sorts of pornography including teen porn. Now that was scary, especially when I had a teenage daughter. I feared heavily for my oldest daughter; I did not know what Jack was capable of doing. I remembered previously catching Jack on several occasions going into my daughter's room while she was not there. We never understood why he visited her room so often. When we questioned him about going in her room, he would always deny it. We knew he was in her room because he would accidentally leave his shoes in her room.

Different people started addressing me about Jack's relationship with my oldest daughter. One minister came to me and said she was concerned about Jack and how he leered at my oldest daughter. Shortly after, my mother had visited us again, and she had noticed the same thing. I asked my daughter if he had ever touched her or stared at her inappropriately. It was a tough question to ask, but I had to. Thank God she said no.

If I can offer some advice, we really need to be mindful, especially when you have several people noticing the same thing. I kind of notice Jack acting strange, but I did not put two and two together until it was brought to my attention. This is definitely a serious issue. When two people are saying the same thing, you do not want to take this matter lightly. Too many times we hear daughters being molested by their fathers or stepfathers. They voice their concerns to their mother, but many times, they are ignored. We tend to accept the man over our children. Then our children grow up with many wounds and scars from sexual abuse as a child. I definitely did not want this to happen to my daughters.

After confronting Jack on the pornography in the house several times, Jack told me he had gotten rid of the pornography for good. A few weeks passed by and everything seemed well. Then, I started having weird dreams. For many nights, I was awakened by these horrible dreams. The dreams were of pornographic women who were trying to attack me in my sleep. This pornography had become spiritual warfare in the house. Normally, when I have dreams like this, there is something in the house that does not belong there.

The next day I went on a search, looking for any ungodly material. Finally, my search came to an end. The last place I would have looked was where I found my answer. Directly above my room was the attic. To enter the attic, you must go through the garage. Since I lived in the home for two years, I had never been in the attic. This was the first for me. I entered the garage and pulled down the stairs that led to the attic. You would not believe what I found. You got it. Pornography galore! The attic was filled with pornographic materials. Jack knew that I would never go in the attic, so this was the best place to hide it. There was pornography stuffed in a cooler and various other inconspicuous places. This monster was bigger than I imagined. Thank God for the Holy Spirit. It was His Spirit that led me in the attic.

I Have Had Enough

Now what? Jack and I were at it again. I told him to remove all of the ungodly material out of the house. Once the materials were completely removed, my peaceful sleep was restored. But that was it. I had enough. It was time for Jack to hit the road. After all of this, I knew for sure it was time to depart from Jack. I had no idea who I married. I was sleeping with the enemy. Everything about Jack began to come to the light.

A few weeks before this incident, Jack and I had visited a church in Oklahoma. During altar call, we had walked up for prayer. Before we made it to the altar, there was a minister with his hands stretch out, directing us in his direction. As we walked up, the minister told my husband that he had a word from the Lord for him. Keep in mind; we did not know this guy at all. This was the first time we had seen him. The minister stared at my husband and said, "Your family needs you emotionally, physically, and spiritually. Your family needs your help."

There were so many ways that God was trying to get through to Jack. It does not matter how many times God speaks to us. We still have to make the decision to change. No matter what, Jack refused to change. I just knew after he heard the word from the Lord, he would get his ducks in line. Nope! He was content with his lifestyle. Honestly, throughout the whole marriage Jack never changed; his actions only became worse. Even when the Lord had warned Jack, he still turned his back on the Word. So I knew that the time was drawing near, and God would soon provide the answer that I had been waiting for: *Lord Save My Marriage or Lord Save My Life.*

I prayed to the Lord for direction of what to do. I knew our lives were at stake. After I prayed, there was a peace that came over me. For the first time, the peace of God had given me a release from my husband. After God gave me peace to separate from Jack, we moved into our separate homes. It was now up to Jack to choose life and pursue God. Up to this point, I had followed God's footsteps and done all I could do. My next direction from the Lord was to stand.

I have fought a good fight, I have finished my course, I have kept the faith. (II Timothy 4:7)

From the time I turned my marriage over to the Lord, I followed God's direction. My desire was to do everything to reconcile the marriage. First, I looked inwardly to make sure there was nothing I was doing that hindered our marriage from prospering. Then I crucified my flesh and began to walk in love. However, I realized that I could not change Jack. We cannot change people. The decision is totally up to that person.

I walked with God from the beginning to the finish line. I had finished my course. The ball was in Jack's court. It was up to him if he wanted a spirit-filled marriage, or he wanted to continue to live his life in sin.

Naked

A few nights after Jack left, the Lord gave me a dream. In the dream, I was looking at a woman who was hurt and naked with no clothes on. This woman sat on the edge of her bed in despair with her head drooped down. That woman was me. As my head hung down, Jack walked out the bedroom for the final time, saying his last goodbyes.

The next morning when I awoke, the Lord brought the dream back to my memory. What stood out the most in the dream was my nakedness. For some reason, I really needed to understand more about the nakedness. I sought out advice

from one of my spiritual fathers. He explained to me that nakedness denotes without covering. The Lord showed me that
His covering and blessing was no longer over my marriage.
I'm sure God wanted to bless our marriage, but Jack never let
go of serving other gods.

When God placed Adam and Eve in the garden, they were
naked and not ashamed. Their marriage was blessed, and God
was in covenant with them. Under one condition, God commanded them to not eat from the tree of knowledge (good and
evil). As long as they ate from the tree of life, they would continue to live in prosperity. Shortly after God had commanded
them to not eat from the tree of knowledge, Eve ate fruit from
the tree of knowledge and shared some with Adam. That moment, God's covering was removed from their lives, and he was
no longer obligated to provide for them.

> Whatever the exact nature of this tree – literal, figurative,
> or symbolic – the essence of Adam and Eve's sin was this:
> they wanted to transfer control of their lives from God to
> themselves. God had, in substance, told them they could
> do anything they wanted to, *except* for that one thing. As
> long as they were in right relationship with God – in other
> words, as long as they recognized God as their creator and
> master – they experienced life as God had intended it to
> be, and they were truly the crown of God's creation. They
> were completely satisfied with this life until Satan, in the
> form of a serpent, deceived them into thinking that if they
> were like God and knew what he knows, life would be even
> better. Once the seed of deception had been planted, they
> became dissatisfied. (Halley's Bible Handbook, 91)

I ate from the tree of knowledge the day I chose to marry

Jack. When I made the decision to marry, I took control of my own life and decisions. Just like Halley explained, the seed of deception (God is not going to send me a husband, so I must find one on my own or my biological clock is running out) was planted, and I became dissatisfied. As a result of all of this, I found myself naked and ashamed. Soon this dream will come more to light as the days continued.

A few days after the dream, God spoke to my spirit and told me to visit Jack's house. This was unlike me. I tried as much as possible to stay away from his house, allowing him the opportunity to receive God for himself. Going over to Jack's house was the last place I wanted to go, but the Lord kept tugging on my heart to go over to his house. Finally, I got in to my vehicle and headed over to Jack's house. The whole time I was driving I was questioning God. I kept asking God "Why am I going over to his house? You know I do not want to go over to his house. Am I going to see a woman or something?" Sure enough when I got to Jack's house there was a woman in his house. They had both been drinking and was consumed heavily with alcohol. It was a pitiful sight to see. I could not believe my eyes. We were not even separated for 2 weeks. How did this happen?

When Jack met this woman, he had stop visiting his daughter. He said he did not want to hurt his new girlfriend's feelings. How does that sound? I'm his wife, and that's his girlfriend. His response really should not surprise you by now. I dealt with this from the moment I said "I do" until now.

My course was finished. It was up to Jack to make a difference in his own life. God told me in Florida that I had not considered Him in the decision process. From then on, I had turned my life over to Him and waited for the answer. Was this the answer I was looking for? No, it was not. God shone the light in the midst of the darkness.

When you think about the process of time from the beginning of my marriage to the end, you can see that there was a promise stage, a process stage, and a performance stage.

1. Promise Stage: God said He would set me free. I did not know how He was going to do it. I just believed and followed His word.

2. Process Stage: Believe the promise no matter what the circumstances were.

3. Performance Stage: See the promise come to pass.

Have faith that God would perform that which He promised. Therefore, "I staggered not at the promises of God through unbelief; but was strong in faith, giving glory to God; and being fully persuaded that, what he had promised, He was able also to perform (Romans 4:20-21, emphasis added).

When I started writing this book, I had no idea what the end of the story would be like. Of course, I thought my marriage would be saved. I wanted the happy ending, but it did not happen. I asked God to save my marriage, but he chose to save my life instead. Through all my suffering and many tears, God promised me that my "weeping may endure for a night, but joy cometh in the morning" (Psalm 30:5).

As you go through the process, know that you are not alone. God is with you every step of the way. God led me through the process until He gave me an answer. It took a while, but it was worth the wait. Because I waited on the Lord and allowed

Him to direct my path, now I know that "there is therefore now no condemnation to them which are in Christ Jesus, who walk not after the flesh, but after the Spirit" (Romans 8:1). I do not feel guilty because I know without a shadow of doubt, God released me.

My joy came. It did not come the way I wanted it to come, but it came the way God intended for my life. The person I married was not God's best for my life. If he was, I honestly believe we would still be together today. After my husband committed adultery, I chose to divorce. My life of freedom had begun.

For me, it was a saved life and a saved family. God does not call us to an abusive relationship. He gave His son, Jesus, just so you could live. So why would He choose death for you. That is a lie from the enemy. Satan's goal is to kill you. Whether he kills you emotionally, physically or spiritually, it does not matter. When the enemy thought he had me down, God lifted me up and shaped me back into the person He called me to be from the beginning. Remember, at the end of your race there is a prize that waits for you. My prize was a saved life from an abusive marriage that almost cost me my life.

God will walk you to your answer. You just have to be willing to go all the way. Do not give up on your marriage. Although you may experience some bumps and bruises along the way, you must keep going until God says otherwise. You must hold on and wait on your answer from the Lord. You never know, *your marriage could be a miracle waiting to happen.*

THE PERFORMANCE

A PRIZE AWAITS

A t the end of the race, there is a blessing waiting for you. The ultimate goal is to keep going until you receive the prize. To receive your reward, you have to "press toward the mark for the prize of the high calling of God in Christ Jesus" (Philippians 3:14). Many times, we stop before we receive the blessing and leave God standing and waiting to give us the prize. We should not permit any obstacles to stop us. We have to keep pressing forward, allowing nothing to hinder us from the prize. We have to literally see ourselves running a race and crossing the finish line.

Let's do a small exercise. Close your eyes for 30 seconds and see yourself running a race. Now, see yourself crossing the finish line and receiving the prize. The same way you just visualized yourself running the race and received a prize is the same way you have to see yourself in life: a winner. "…Christ always leads us in triumph [as trophies of Christ's victory]" (II

Corinthians 2:14, AMP). It does not matter what place you come in. The blessing is promised to anyone who finishes the race. The race is not to the swift, but it is to the ones who endure to the end (Ecclesiastes 9:11). If you stop, you will never receive your prize with your name on it.

What prize will you receive at the end of the race? The prize could be your marriage being restored. The prize could be God bringing you closer to Him through your experiences. The prize could be God removing you out of an adulterous relationship. The prize could be God removing you out of an abusive relationship. Whatever prize God has for you, it is for you. Sometimes we are not satisfied with the prize God has for us. We do not want to listen to His answers, so we ignore Him and go on about our business.

There was a story about a little boy who had a bird in a cage. One day, he decided to let the bird fly away to see if it would come back to him. He said that if the bird comes back to him, it was always his. On the other hand, if the bird does not return, it was never his. You have to prepare yourself for the outcome. If the bird never returns, you have to let go. God knows what is best for you. He is not trying to take something from you. He is trying to get something to you: LIFE.

All relationships are not good for us. Just like all foods are not good for us. There are certain foods that may taste good, but they are harmful to our bodies. Likewise, some relationships seem good, but they are altogether physically, emotionally and spiritually bad for us. If it is meant to be, it will be. If it is not meant to be, then God will cause that person to be removed from your life. The Bible speaks of a woman in First Samuel 25, named Abigail. Abigail was described as "a woman of good understanding, and of a beautiful countenance." On the other hand, her husband, Nabal, was described as "churlish (rude) and evil in his doings...such a wicked man that no one could talk to him." Although, her husband was a very wicked man, she was still loyal to him. At one time, she even interceded for her husband, so David would not take his life. She understood that we do not have to repay evil for evil, and God will fight our battles. Because of her husband's wickedness, 10 days later after she pleaded with David to not kill him, the Lord struck Nabal and he died. Abigail completely turned her situation over to the Lord. It was God who removed him from her life. And shortly after his death, she was married to a man who was soon to be king, David. Of course, you do not want anything drastic, at least I hope and pray you do not, to happen to your spouse, *but* when God is in control, He does everything according to His will.

Let God separate the wheat from the tare and determine the prize at the end of your race (Matthew 13:30). Regardless of the prize at the end of the race, we are all still winners.

I highly encourage you to finish the race and accept the prize that God has for you.

10

AFTER THE STORM

When God released me from my marriage, initially I did not want to leave. Immediately, fear and doubt rose up in me. I feared that people would look at me differently as a single mother with two children. Prior to marriage, I understood what it was like to be a single mother. Unfortunately, it was the church folks who ostracized singles. That was one of my biggest fears. What would Christian people think about me being a single parent and working in the ministry? How would I explain the divorce? The ones who should have been merciful and loving as God had called us to be were the ones who I feared the most (religious church folks).

Before I got married, I endured the abuse, especially by married women. Either singles were classified as husband or wives' snatchers or something was wrong with them. Most singles would tell you that there is nothing wrong with them; they are blessed and highly favored. The truth of the matter is that they are patiently waiting on the Lord to fulfill whatever their desires may be just like everyone else. Some people decided not to wait on God, particularly in marriage relationships and now the divorce rates are extremely high. It is important to continue in the work of ministry while you wait for God's best. Habakkuk 2:3 says, "Though it linger, wait for it; it will certainly come and will not delay" (NIV).

In many occasions, singles are looked down upon. Jay E. Adams, speaks on this same issue in his book titled *Marriage, Divorce, and Remarriage in the Bible* (10). Adams says:

> Christian singles ought not to be looked down upon by marrieds or neglected (as so often they are). Rather, they ought to be honored for the special efforts they make in pursuit of the special kingdom tasks to which God has called them. That doesn't mean pinning medals on them, but it does mean conferring honor on those to whom honor is due. After all, Paul was one of those special people; we do not look down on him do we?

We look at Apostle Paul as a legend and never questioned his status. Why is it that we question the singles in the church today?

Paula Sandford, who is a co-founder of Elijah House Ministries, "has ministered to countless number of women in the areas of inner healing and transformation as an ordained minister and counselor." She mentions in her book, *Healing for a Woman's Emotions*:

> What is so tragic is that, far too often, singles in the church who were married and are now divorced feel like outcasts. They are made to feel as if they have committed an unforgivable sin. And the church has put limitations on them,

especially in the area of ministry.

Hence the reason I was afraid to divorce. I assumed the church would put limitation on my ministry and would judge me based on my status. I almost allowed the thoughts of others to keep me bound in my marriage. Although this perception was found to be true in some churches, that is not the case in all churches. They are some spirit-filled churches who do not judge your past or your status. Instead, they acknowledge the gift of God operating inside of you. Thank God for churches who do not hold your past over your head.

Because of the thoughts of other Christians, I was going to choose a life of pornography, adultery, depression, suicide and possible sexual abuse of my children over a life of freedom. As long as I held on to do those negative thoughts, there was nothing that God could do. In order to live a purpose driven life ordained by God, I had to begin "Casting down imaginations, and every high thing that exalteth itself against the knowledge of God, and bringing into captivity every thought to the obedience of Christ" (2 Corinthians 10:5).

Thoughts of others can really affect your decision. During the same time I was going through my divorce, I met a single father who was also going through a divorce. His wife decided she did not want to be with him anymore. He found out later that she had another man on the side and became pregnant by him, while they were still married. It was amazing to see that although she was pregnant by another man, he was still willing to take her back. However, she refused his request. As a result, he was in his final stages of his divorce. He mentioned that being a single father of four children and an assistant pastor had been a challenge. One of his biggest obstacles was how people viewed him. He really felt like his divorce and his status (single father) would hold him back in the ministry. This young man allowed his thoughts to get the best of him, and he was already looking for another wife before his divorce was final. To my surprise, this man remarried a year after his divorce.

Exactly what this guy was facing, I was dealing with in my own life and allowed it to almost hold me back. I felt like pastors and other Christians would judge me if I got a divorce. I was like a prisoner. God released me from prison (abusive marriage), but my thoughts kept me in captivity. Sometimes we cannot see ourselves living successfully outside of our marriages, and we continue to live in bondage. What is really in bondage is our mind. Joyce Meyers hit it right on the nose when she said, "The battlefield of the mind." Instead of renewing our mind to God's purpose for our lives, we focus on fear and unbelief. We refuse to see ourselves outside of bondage, so we choose death over life. That's the same mentality the children of Israel had. They were in bondage for so long they could not understand freedom. That's why in the middle of their journey to the promise land they wanted to go back. They would rather go back to physical, spiritual, and mental abuse than choose God's perfect will. They became accustomed to their environment.

However, there comes a time in our life when we have to count our losses and move on. It is not worth it for a male or female to stay in an abusive relationship. God did not ordain you to live in an abusive relationship. That is not the kind of God we serve. We serve a loving and kind God who only wants the best for you. God sent His love (Jesus Christ) to set us free from oppression. Therefore, it is not His will to put you in a bad relationship to teach you a lesson. His plans are not to harm us.

For I know the plans I have for you, declares the Lord, plans to prosper you and not to harm you, plans to give you hope and a future. (Jeremiah 29:11, NIV)

God wants to give you a hope and a future. If God said it, so be it. You must trust God and walk in faith. I was challenged with the same decision, dreading the end of my marriage. Although fear rose in me, I did not allow it to overtake me. I chose the abundant life and obeyed the voice of the Lord.

Restoration

Because of my obedience, God has restored everything I lost and replaced my tears with joy. Keep in mind, everything we go through in life is a process. Restoration and healing is a process, and it takes time. But rest assure, your joy will come and your latter days will be greater.

I have been blessed beyond measure. Since my divorce, my life and ministry have exploded. I have experienced the best years of my life. I am no longer financially, emotionally, spiritually, and physically depressed. I have bought a home, and God has provided finances for my oldest daughter to go to college and my youngest daughter to go to a private school. Now that is God! He has really blessed my life all around. On top of that, God has given me the opportunity to speak at conferences, other churches, direct a women's ministry and write this book to help someone else come out of bondage. I have gone places I never thought I could have gone. God replaced my fears with His love. No longer do I have a "spirit of fear, but of power, and of love, and of a sound mind" (II Timothy 1:7). The devil is a liar and the truth is not in him and never will be. God can use you no matter what people say or think.

Encouragement

To you reading this book right now, I encourage you to stay strong in the Lord and trust Him to direct your path. You *can* go on in life. I am a living testimony. The same Jesus that lives inside me is inside you. What God has done for me He will do for you. Every day we have to make a decision: choose life or death. The bible says in Deuteronomy 30:19:

> *This day I call heaven and earth as witnesses against you that I have set before you life and death, blessings and curses. Now choose life, so that you and your children may live and that you may love the Lord your God, listen to his voice, and hold fast to him. For the Lord is your life, and he will give you many years in the land he swore to give to your fathers, Abraham, Isaac, and Jacob (NIV).*

God sets life and death before us each day. You have to make the decision for your life. I chose life, so that my children and I would live. Before Moses died, one of his last and most profound speeches included these words: "Now choose life." He did not say choose life tomorrow or next year. Moses said if you choose life today and as a result, you would no longer be under a curse. You will be able to love the Lord even more, you will listen to the voice of the Lord, and you will hold fast to him. The words that Moses spoke are the very words that saved my life. Because I choose life over death, today I LIVE.

I pray that you will hear the voice of the Lord and choose life. If God did not tell you to move, by all means, do not move until you hear the voice of the Lord.

He's Faithful and Just to Forgive

It is ok to recognize where you are in the process. You may ask yourself, why was I so stupid? Why I did not listen to God? I should have known better. Whether we made a stupid decision or not, God has set us free from all condemnation. He has brought you out to bring you in to His unfailing love. "There is none righteous, no, not one" (Romans 3:10). So do not be down on yourself, "For all have sinned, and come short of the glory of God" (Romans 3:23). There were many men and women in the Bible who messed up the first time before they eventually got it right.

For example, look at King David's life. David committed adultery *and* murdered the woman's husband to cover up what he did. That was not the greatest decision. However, notice that through his failures in life, God did not leave David. God was there before, during, and after his wilderness experience. Granted, David had to suffer the consequences for his bad decision, but it did not stop him from being a man after God's own heart. God picked him back up and started him on the right track.

God loves us through our good and bad decisions. Our choices do not stop God from being who He is. God is love, and there is no sin too big that God cannot forgive. The only sin he will not forgive is the one you are not willing to admit. He says, "If we confess our sins, he is faithful and just to forgive us our sins, and to cleanse us from all unrighteousness" (I John 1:9). Therefore, lift up your eyes, and hold your head up high. God has "given unto you beauty for ashes, the oil of joy for mourning, the garment of praise for the spirit of heaviness" (Isaiah 61:3, emphasis added).

It is time for restoration. Allow God to love you, heal your wounds and build you back up. Embrace your future with God. As long as you walk with God daily, He will not allow you to fall and make the wrong decisions.

Begin to live your new life of freedom in God. Recognize "...where the Spirit of the Lord is, there is freedom."

WHAT NOW

A fter having gone through many of the experiences I explained throughout this book, I can now see the wisdom that the Lord has given me. Now as a single mother in ministry, I know what trusting, believing and obeying God is like, even when it hurts. Experiencing pain is a great indicator that something is dying. I believe all along God has been trying to kill us so that He can live through us.

Maybe you are just coming out of an abusive marriage or maybe you are still in one or maybe you are single and thinking of settling for someone that you know God has not purposed for your life. Wherever you are, I believe God has some wisdom He wants to share with you before you make any major decisions. I am sure there is more, but I have found seven major keys to remember when seeking God for direction in marital relationships.

1. **Wait Before You Say I Do:** If you wait long enough, God will show you if the person is for you or not. Do not think that God has passed you by. He has not forgotten. If you do not have a potential mate at this moment in your life, it means that God does not have one ready for you now. If He brought the person now, they would not be ready. Therefore, do not rush and find someone and then later regret your decision.

   The best thing to do is wait on the Lord and refuse to settle for less. You deserve God's best and not the world's best. God holds the key to your future husband or wife and when He is ready to unlock the door, He will release your future spouse. When God does it, you will avoid unnecessary suffering.

Statistics shows that over 50% of Christian marriages end up in a divorce. That means that at least 1 out of every 2 couples who walk down the aisle will end up in a divorce. Why is this? In most cases, we marry for the wrong reasons. We did not allow God to join our marriages together.

2. **Get Rooted In The Word:** If you have recently received Christ as your Lord and Savior, I suggest you get rooted in the Word before you even think about marriage. This is a vulnerable time in your walk with God. As soon as you are saved, the enemy tries to throw many things in your direction.

   I learned just because someone says they are saved does not mean they are saved. You have to have the spirit of discernment and wisdom to determine if the person really loves the Lord. Get rooted in the Word, so you can "beware of false prophets, which come to you in sheep's clothing, but inwardly they are ravening wolves" (Matthew 7:15).

When my husband and I got married, I was a baby Christian. There were many things I did not know about the Word of God, so I was deceived. If I knew what I know now, I would not have made some of the mistakes I did. Because of my bad decisions, I had to suffer the consequences.

3. **Seek Christian Counseling:** Be sure the counselor is a reputable person. This person should give you sound doctrine based on the Word of God. Usually they are trained to ask questions that you do not think to ask.

   This will give you the opportunity to know more about the person and their relationship with God. You can then iron out any disagreements or differences before the marriage. Then you can better decide if this is the person you want to spend the rest of your life with.

   For the ones who are already married, I suggest you find a Christian counselor that both parties can agree with. If one person does not want to go, I suggest the other person seeks counseling alone. This will help you grow in your relationship with God and build your faith and trust in Him.

Jesus said, "Anyone who listens to my teachings and obeys me is wise, like a person who builds a house on a solid rock. Though the rain comes in torrents and the floodwaters rise and the winds beat against that house, it will not collapse, because it is built on a rock. But anyone who hears my teaching and ignores it is foolish, like a person who builds a house on sand. When the rains and floods come and the winds beat against that house, it will fall with a mighty crash" (Matthew 7:24-27, NLT).

4. **Do Not Settle for the 50% Rule:** The 50% rule is accepting 50% of what you want (a man or a woman) and accepting the other 50% of the person you do not want (secret life that involves, pornography, drugs, alcohol, homosexuality, anger, and/or financial irresponsibility etc).

   When you have a relationship that does not have all the fruit of the spirit (Read Galatians 5:22-23), you see the form of godliness, but everything else about God and His great power is denied. That person is going to have a form of godliness. It is like only obeying some of the Word, but not all of it.

   Do not settle. You want a woman or man that is complete. If you compromise the 50% to have someone, then later on in your marriage you going to regret the other 50% that you accepted with the package. It is either all or none.

There is a woman I know, who is a minister, who desperately desired a husband. She dated this guy who was active in the church, but at the same time, he visited the bars and drank occasionally. She satisfied the 50% she wanted by marrying this man. Guess what! When she married that man, she married his drinking and his going out to the bars. She got more than the 50% that was "good". She accepted the whole package!

When you go to a dealership, there are many vehicles you can choose from. You can get a vehicle with no special amenities. This type of vehicle normally lacks air conditioning, cruise control, automatic windows and locks. On the other hand, you can choose the vehicle that is fully loaded. This is normally the top of the line kind of vehicle. In the Kingdom, that is the type of husband or wife you want: Someone who is fully loaded with the Word of God and living the God-kind of lifestyle (physically, emotionally, financially, and spiritually). You want a 100% godly woman or man. If you choose the vehicle that's plain and stripped from the other necessities, then that's all you are going to get.

5. **Understand the Person's Past:** Find out as much as you can about the person's past before you marry. You do not have to do a Federal Background Investigation; however, you want to find out as much as possible about the person. This will help you understand your future spouse and why they act and react the way they do.

   See how he or she handles family relationships and finances. When God joins a couple together, He brings prosperity in every area and not poverty. This is so important.

Recently, God took me back to Jack's family situation growing up and showed me how it affected our relationship. The Lord showed me how his upbringing affected him as a man and husband. Jack grew up in a home with his mother and his father. Most of Jack's life, his father was not home. His father had a relationship with another woman whom he lived with for more than 20 years. Throughout Jack's childhood, his father was in between both homes. Jack was fully aware of his father's actions. At a very young age, they learned to accept his father's behavior.

Through all of this, Jack's mother never divorced her husband. Each night she would pray to the Lord that he would bring her husband back home. Eventually after Jack grew up and moved out of the house, his father received the Lord and came back to live with his mom. God restored their relationship.

How does learning about Jack's childhood experiences play into my marriage? Well, as a child, Jack did not have a godly father figure. The only example he had was his father living with another woman, and his mother accepted this behavior. During this time, his father did not help out with the finances.

Have you ever heard of the saying whatever the monkey sees the monkey will do? Well, in the Kingdom of God, it is called a generational curse. Because of his father's relationship with his mother, Jack followed his father's footsteps. That was the only example he had. Jack lived what he had learned as a child in our marriage. "He was in and out the house. There were nights he did not come home. He did not support the family or help pay the bills. And he had relations with other women." Now, that explains why he stayed with his friends countless nights without calling home. Jack had no stability whatsoever.

At the same time, while he was learning from his father, he also learned from his mother, that was to stay with your husband no matter what the circumstances (life or death), and God will bring him back to you. It explains that when I wanted a divorce, even though Jack had another woman, He would compare me to his mother. He would say, "My mother did not leave my father for 20 something years when he left the house. She was a true woman of God." In other words, his mother accepted the abuse; therefore, I should do the same.

To avoid making the wrong decision that can cost you your life, please know the person you are about to marry. Know where he or she comes from and where they are going in Christ.

6. **Understand Your Past:** Out of all things I mentioned, I believe this is the most important one. It is just as important to understand your past as it is to understand another person's past. To discover things about yourself can be sometimes quite difficult. In most cases, we do not want to do a self-evaluation. We would rather use the pronoun "you" rather than "I". It is hard to speak in first person because it hits too close to home, but you must understand yourself. When you find out who you are, it is easy to understand why you choose and do the things that you do.

   Before God can use us, we must be willing to tell Him all about us and admit all of our sins. Once you lay out your dirty laundry, no one, not even the enemy can use your past against you. A self-evaluation will stop you from making the same mistakes over and over again.

For instance, I chose my husband based on my past. I was looking for love in all the wrong places and tried to live up to my family's name. Now, that I realize what triggered me to do what I did in the past, I do not allow these things to affect me anymore.

It was not until after the Samaritan woman (John 4) revealed her past that God was able to set her free and deliver her once and for all. Until you face your past, you cannot embrace your future and the things that God has in store for you.

7. **It Is Not Your Job to Raise Them:** We think we are doing them a favor, but we are doing more harm than good. Women are naturally born to nurture. Often times, we try to nurture our husbands into the man we desire them to be. In this case, we take the role of God and try to change them. Anytime you try to change a person, you are operating in witchcraft.

I met a woman one day who thought she was helping her husband become a better person. This woman's encouragement turned into discouragement. She was running her husband further away from God. Well, I thought the same thing. I thought I was helping my spouse. The only thing I was doing was causing more frustration in his life. Why? I could not get him to change and do what I wanted him to do. The problem with us ladies is sometimes we treat our husbands like our child, and we get mad when they will not change or hearken to our voice.

You can hang it up. That man is not going to change at your command. If so, his change will only be evident from the outside, but his heart will remain the same. We have to allow God to make the changes in the person's heart. Therefore, the change is permanent and not temporary.

Remember, your voice is a voice of a stranger. A sheep only follows the voice of the Shepherd. We are not the Shepherd. My best advice is to go to your prayer closet and ask God to manifest changes in your husband life.

This message also applies to the husband as well. You do not have the ability to change your wife. Bottom line… we must trust and depend on God to make the changes in the person's life.

12

SAVED MARRIAGE

One thing I will never tell a person to do is to get a divorce. That decision is between you and God. I am only encouraging you to seek help before it is too late. I will never take the place of God in the decision making process. As far as I know, God could change your spouses' heart and restore your marriage.

There have been abusive marriages restored by God. For instance, there was a woman who truly loved the Lord and devoted her life completely to Him. One night she was on her way to church. Her husband told her if she goes to church he was going to lock her out of the house. Although her husband threatened to lock her out of the house, she did not allow her husband's threats to hinder her from going to church. She proceeded out the door and went to church. When she returned home that night, her husband had locked her out of the house. She quietly slept on the porch all night long. The next morning her husband unlocked the door and let her in.

What was her response? Did she yell at him? Did she ignore him? The answer is none of the above. She peacefully walked into the house and went straight to the kitchen and cooked her husband some breakfast. When her husband saw her reactions, he was stunned. Because of her relationship with Christ and her compassion towards her husband, she won her husband to Christ. Today, her husband is saved, and he is a renowned minister.

It was her act of obedience to God's Word and her compassion that drew her husband to Christ and brought restoration to her marriage. She demonstrated exactly what Apostle Paul said in I Corinthians 7:13-14. "If a Christian woman has a husband who is an unbeliever, and he is willing to continue living with her, she must not leave him. For the Christian wife brings holiness to her marriage" (NLT). This Christian woman did not leave her husband; instead, she allowed her holiness to reconcile her marriage.

It is important that we walk the talk because our obedience can potentially save our marriage. As you can see, if both parties are willing to work towards restoration, God can save your marriage. Just like this woman did, you must continue to walk in love.

Remember, it is not what you say that will draw your spouse to Christ. It is how you live and demonstrate the love of God that will win your spouse to Christ and save your marriage.

Diana Hagee, in her book *What Every Woman Wants In A Man*, gives another example of how God can restore a broken marriage. Diana Hagee expressed that "There were two couples in our church whose families had become close friends.

Through circumstances not ordained by God, the husband of one family and the wife of the other began a torrid sexual affair. Once discovered, we immediately put both couples into counseling, each one proclaiming a desire for reconciliation. Time passed, and healing seemed to occur. More time passed, and the two resumed their affair. Discouraged, yet still hopeful because the offended parties desired to forgive, we led the two couples through counseling once again. However, this time we asked one of the families to leave the church in order to give both families a chance to survive. The couple that stayed in the church began their road to recovery. The offended party had every biblical right to a divorce but chose for the life and not the death of the marriage. The road was long and steep. The road was often tiresome and tedious. But the path of repentance led to healing. This couple is now a prime example of true forgiveness and restoration, and now offers help to those who find themselves in similar situations. This couple is able to give back to others what God has given them – grace, mercy, and restoration" (Diana Hagee, 16).

As far as the couple that left the church, their marriage ended up in a divorce. So by all means, hear the voice of the Lord. Each person or couple has to evaluate their own situation and determine which direction or plan God has for your life or marriage. Either God will save your marriage or save your life. That decision is between you and God.

Meanwhile, if your husband or wife is being abusive and you are losing your mind, your health, and your zeal for Christ, you may need to step back and look closely at the situation. This may be a signal to ask God for clarity and direction for your life.

13

SAVED LIFE

Whenever we have crises in our life and we call on the name of Jesus, he has a need to answer our call. John 4:4 says, "And He (Jesus) must needs go through Samaria" (emphasis added). That day when Jesus departed from Galilee he had a need to go to Samaria. Just as it was important for Jesus to go to Samaria, it is important for Jesus to meet you at your well. He met me. I had thoughts of suicide, and I did not want to continue in life. Through all my ups and downs, there was still something deep down inside of me. It was a miracle waiting to happen. My miracle was disguised as a need. For the miracle to manifest, Jesus had a need to stop at my address and set me free from a marriage that almost cost me my life. I felt like the Samaritan woman at the well.

When Jesus passed through Samaria, he met a Samaritan woman at the well and asked her for a drink. With surprise, the Samaritan woman questioned Jesus and asked, "How is it that thou, being a Jew, askest drink of me, which am a woman of Samaria? For the Jews have not dealings with the Samaritans" (John 4:9).

First off, the woman was surprised that Jesus even talked to her. The Samaritans were considered a mix-race and a disgrace to the Jews, so it was odd for Jesus to have a conversation with her. The Jews were the ones to carry the Gospel of Jesus Christ, but they kept it from the Samaritans. Likewise, the Christians are the ones to carry the Gospel of Jesus Christ to the hurting people of this world, but because of their own personal perceptions of the Bible and divorces; some choose to keep walking without addressing the need.

When I was facing the dilemma in my marriage, it seemed like there was no one to talk to about what was going on in my life. Everyone turned away, and I was on my own. Even though, James 5:14 says, "Is any sick among you? Let him call for the elders of the church; and let them pray over him, anointing him with oil in the name of the Lord". In most cases we cannot find someone to pray or agree with us. Talking about a bad marriage is like talking about an incurable disease. In other words, it does not matter how bad your relationship is or how abusive the person is towards you, God hates divorce and that is the bottom line. He does hates divorce, but he also hates abuse. It is easier to look religiously at Scriptures rather than the true purpose of Jesus' arrival to the earth: to set the captives free.

That is why we find many Christians passing the Samaritan woman by and looking down upon her. Instead of reaching their hands down to her and lifting her up, they held their hands back and pushed her further away from God. That is why you find the woman at the well surprised that Jesus even had the time to come her way.

Imagine how long the Samaritan woman was in her current situation. Her situation was so bad "the woman saith unto Jesus, Sir, I do not have anything to draw with, and my wounds are deep: from where can you find this living water. Are you greater than our father Jacob, which gave us the well, and drank thereof himself, and his children, and his cattle" (John 4:11 – 12, emphasis added)? The woman had nothing else to draw from. She tried everything to fill her void, but she was still incomplete. It was obvious the woman was still looking for help. If not, she would not have asked Jesus where she could find this living water. The woman was desperate for an answer, but previous to her meeting with Jesus she did not know anyone who could provide it.

Jesus answered and said unto her, "Whosoever drinketh of this water shall thirst again, But whosoever drinketh of the water that I shall give him shall never thirst; but the water that I shall give him shall life be in him a well of water springing up into everlasting" (John 4:13-14). Apparently the water she had been drinking was not the water of eternal life. The water she drank was unfulfilling. That is why she kept re-visiting dead-end relationships. She never had a word of life that could bring her out of her situation up until this point. This woman needed a word from God. One word from God can change your life forever.

God met me at my well. When it seemed like all else had failed, God showed up. Just like He showed up for the Samaritan woman, He will show up for you. Once Jesus shows up in our lives, we must be willing to air out our dirty laundry and "tell Him the *truth*, the whole *truth*, and nothing but the *truth*, so help us God." Before God could bring her out of her past mistakes, she had to reveal all the skeletons in her closet.

Jesus saith unto her, "Go, call thy husband, and come hither." The woman answered and said, "I have no husband. Jesus said unto her, Thou hast well said, I have no husband" (John 4:16:17). At this point, her integrity was put on trial. Of course, Jesus knows everything about us, but we must be willing to reveal the truth to Him. When your very life is on the line and you have come to the point where you are sick and tired of being sick and tired, you will begin to tell Jesus everything. I had to admit my past failures and sins to the Lord and asked for forgiveness. That included asking for forgiveness of going into a marriage God did not ordain for my life. I acknowledged my wrongs, and God was faithful and just to forgive me and made me whole again. At the moment of my humility and dependence upon God, He was able to work with me.

After the Samaritan woman freely admits that she has no husband, Jesus said, "For thou hast had five husbands; and he whom thou now hast is not thy husband: in that saidst thou truly" (John 4:18). I have heard various interpretations of this scripture. The woman did indeed have five husbands. However, none of her marriages were approved in God's eyesight. Some interpret that the woman had adultery with five men and so forth. If that was the case, then why would Jesus say, "Thou hast had five husbands; and he whom thou now hast is not thy husband" (John 4:18)? I believe that Jesus was referencing her choice of husbands. Yes, she was married, but the marriages were not ordained by God but by man (self-will). Since the woman was never revealed to the truth, she found herself choosing the wrong choice of men. Until, the light of this world was revealed on her darkness, she lived in bondage.

I have learned that you can be married in the natural, but never married in the Spirit. I was bound to a marriage contract, but never had a husband. The day Jesus met me at the well was the day I was set free and my need became a miracle. The same happened for the Samaritan woman: her needs was transformed into a miracle. When Jesus picked her up, set her free and delivered her soul (mind, will and emotions), for the first time, she was able to worship the Lord in spirit and in truth. Afterwards, she went out in the city and preached to all the people in the town. Because of her testimony, many believed on the Lord that same day. After her divine appointment at the well, this woman had gifts and callings that had not been activated. She had the ability to preach and teach and brought a whole city to believe on the name of Jesus.

Since my experience at the well, the Lord has blessed me in leaps and bounds. I have served God more than ever in the ministry all around. As long as I stayed in a marriage that was not ordained by God, it was difficult to continue further in the ministry. I thank God for what He has done in my life. When no one else would listen, God would.

God Saved My Life

Through all of the things I suffered in my life, I am proud to say I am still standing and by the grace of God I am here today. There is no word in the dictionary that can express my thanks and love towards God for saving my life. That is why I keep thanksgiving in my heart and praise on my lips for what

God has done for me. That is why I praise Him the way I do. There is no one who can tell me that I made the wrong decision. I heard the voice of the Lord, and He led me out of the wilderness straight into His loving arms. I am truly His sheep, and I know and obey His voice.

When Jesus meets you at the well, remember this. There are only two people present at this meeting: You and God. Jesus spoke to the Samaritan woman after His disciples left. Your experience with God is between you and Him alone. Therefore, when someone questions me about my decision to divorce, I tell them:

> "You were not there when Jesus met me at the well and He told me that He loved me. You were not there when He grabbed my hands and promised me that I would be safe in His arms. You were not there when my daughter stopped breathing, and God brought her back to life. You were not there when we did not have any food in the house, and God supplied all of our needs. You were not there when my husband was gone for nights and weeks and the Holy Spirit became my Comforter. You were not there when my husband had pornography that included teens, and I was afraid for the sake of my children. You were not there when my husband told me that he would watch me suffer. You were not there when I caught him with another woman in the bed. You were not there when I became so weak God picked me up and carried me."

I cannot help but to praise Him and thank God for saving me and my family's life. Quite often we desire a saved marriage. God chose to save my life.

14

HOW DID I END UP HERE

If you are going through some major issues in your marriage, my first suggestion is to take a look back over your life and decisions and determine how you ended up in your present situation. Second, I would ask, "Did God join my marriage?" In some cases, we may find ourselves in marriages God did not join together.

For instance, some marriages were established based on pregnancy. They chose to marry for the sake of the child. In other cases, some people got married with the notion the other person would probably change after marriage. Additionally, there were individuals who married who were unsaved and neither one of them knew the Lord.

There are many reasons why people get married. You have to determine if your marriage was set up by God or set up by man. When answering this question, you have to be honest with yourself. While researching your answer, you may find out that God was not the center of your decision to marry. Does that mean He cannot restore your marriage? Absolutely not! God can restore and have mercy on whatever He desires. There are many marriages God has saved. In these marriages, both parties had to work towards a healthy relationship. It takes determination on both sides in order for the marriage to work.

However, there are times when God knows there is no hope for reconciliation. For the sake of your life, He will honor your decision to divorce, especially, if the marriage was not ordained by Him from the beginning. This does not mean to put away your wife or husband for the sake of just doing so. Every decision we make must line up with the Word of God.

What God hates about divorces is the pain it creates in the lives of others. If anyone knows the pain of a divorce, God knows best. God said in Jeremiah 3:8, "I gave faithless Israel her certificate of divorce and sent her away because of all her adulteries" (NIV). Imagine how painful that was for our very own Father. A people who He created for His glory had turned their back on him. Even though God divorced Israel, He never stopped loving them.

If you have been divorced or contemplating divorce, God will continue to love you and forgive you. Some people preach as if divorce is an unforgivable sin, and God will hate you for the rest of your life. In Romans 9:15 the Lord says to Moses, "I will have mercy on whom I have mercy, and I will have compassion on whom I have compassion." The same way God has mercy and compassion, the church should demonstrate the same mercy and compassion for people who have divorced. Besides, it is not like a person wakes up one day and says "I feel like getting a divorce." I'm sure the day when you got married, the last thought on your mind was divorce. God never intended for divorce. It was Moses who wrote the bill of divorcement because of the hardness of one's heart. In most cases, it was sin that led up to a divorce.

Paula Sandford says, "I strongly believe that God Himself can (and surely may) choose, in His mercy, to asunder what men and women in their naïveté or foolishness have only thought to put together. I would further suggest that when repentance is real and forgiveness has been given by the Lord, He may also grant His grace for new beginning."

Never believe that God calls us to an abusive marriage. I say this because so many people are living silently in abusive relationships. Either they have been beaten several times or mentally or emotionally abused. Some have chosen to stay because of other people's convictions.

Answer this. Why would God cause for a man or woman to abuse someone He created in His own likeness and image? This concept does not line up with the Word of God. We cannot allow what other people think dictate what we do and do not do. These are decisions that could cost us our very life. I am sure there are many who have been beaten to death or hospitalized because someone made them feel bad about their decisions.

Listen. You have to obey the voice of the Lord. If God tells you to go, you need to go for the sake of your life and or your children. However, if God tells you to stay in your marriage, then you must stay.

God did not create us to go through life in Hell. That is the very reason He sent Jesus. We were being run over by the devil, and we did not have a way out. God sent Jesus to conquer death. When He did that, our lives were set free and death no longer had control over us.

Now, there is no condemnation to those who are in Christ Jesus (Romans 8:1). God never condemns us. To be condemned means there is no way out. There is a way out. Your way out is through Christ Jesus. God loves you, and He no longer wants you to take any abuse.

He is a Redeemer, Someone who rescues a person from a place where they cannot help themselves. God will rescue you for the sake of your life and or your children lives. That is what He has done for me. He knew that I was in a situation that could cost me my life. Instead of allowing the enemy to destroy me, God became the Lifter of my head.

The only thing God requires for us to do is make sure we do everything we can to bring reconciliation in our marriage. After doing everything that God requires us to do and the person does not change or does not discontinue the abuse, I suggest you continue to pray unto the Lord and ask for direction. "The steps of a good man are ordered (fixed) by the Lord: and He delighteth in his way" (Psalm 37:23 emphasis added).

How you ended up in your current situation does not determine your destiny. The most important thing is finding out God's plans for your marriage and or life and what steps you should take next in the process. As you submit to the Lord, He will lead you to your destiny.

15

FINAL WORDS

I just want to take this opportunity to say, "Thank you" to all of the readers. I truly hope this book has been an inspiration for you. I pray that your life will never be the same. Even though the Lord spoke to me to write this book, I had to keep pressing forward to see it completed. At one point, I even put the book aside assuming that God did not want me to continue forward. But once God kept sending people in my direction who needed ministry and encouragement in their marriages, I realized God still had a plan for this book. Out of the blue, people would come up to me and say, "You will write a great book that's going to set a lot of people free." I pray that this book has done just that for you.

In the bookstore, you will find most books instructing you to follow these 10 steps to a marriage you always desired. But what happens when we follow all 10 steps and our situation remains the same? How do we minister to those folks who had tried all 10 steps, but yet, they are still without an answer? How can we reach that person sitting on the couch who is contemplating suicide? How can we tell a person that God can make them whole all over again? How can we tell a person that they can still live even after a divorce? How can we tell a person that God can save your marriage or your life?

That's one of the reason I wrote this book. We have to remember that we are human, and what works for one does not necessarily mean that it will work for the next person. This does not mean their principles are wrong. It only means that God may have another direction for your deliverance. Too many times we try all the steps and still our situation has not changed. Then we wonder "What did I do wrong?" It does not mean you did something wrong. Maybe God has another plan for your deliverance.

For instance, two people may live in the same household, but they both choose different routes to get home. Did one person do something right and the other person did something wrong?" Absolutely Not! They both chose different direction, but they still ended up at the same address. Therefore, do not be disappointed if one way does not work for you. Just pray and ask God which direction He desires for you to take.

My desire is your prayers are answered through this book, and many marriages and lives are set free. As I was going through my process, I could not find anyone who would tell me how to get from point A to point B. They would only tell me to trust God. There was no one willing to share their testimony. Because of that, many marriages and or lives are in bondage.

My continuous prayer is that God will set the captives free, and He will restore your true purpose for living. I pray that God has given you another level of faith, hope and love and that you will allow him to make the final decision for your destiny: whether it's a saved marriage or a saved life.

Questions

These questions have been added so that you may think more about where you are in your singleness or marriage. The goal is to look at yourself and determine your maturity or your need for healing, restoration, or deliverance. You can answer these questions individually or use for group discussions.

Chapter 1: In the Beginning

1. Do you have a relationship with the Lord?
2. If you had to describe yourself to someone who didn't know you, what would you say?
3. Have you ever identified yourself with family traits? If so, how has it affected who you are?
4. Are you currently in any relationships that are hindering your relationship with God?
5. Are your relationships feeding your flesh or feeding your spirit?

Chapter 2: Rededication

1. What are your motives for getting married?
2. Did you receive pre-marital counseling?
3. Are there any red flags?
4. Did God, self, or others (family, friends, mom, dad, etc) convince you to get married?
5. How well do you know the person you are married to or soon to marry?

6. Does he/she have a relationship with God? If so, explain.

Chapter 3: Through the Valley

1. Have you ever been in a relationship where someone said or showed you one thing, but lived another? What did you do with the relationship?

2. If you are currently dating, do you believe he or she is God's best for you?

3. If you are currently dating, does he or she confess Christ Jesus as Lord? If so, does he or she have the fruit to prove that He is Lord?

4. Are you in a situation where no matter what you do or say, there seems to be no change? If so, have you tried to reach out to someone who can help?

5. Are you holding any unforgiveness in your heart? If so, what is it about? Can you begin to forgive him or her? (You may need someone to help you with this process).

Chapter 4: Change Begins with You

1. Are you trying to change your spouse? Or are you allowing God to make the changes?

2. Why is it better for God to change a person's heart than for you to make the person change?

3. Do you look first to God or man to supply your needs?

4. Have you ever felt like you couldn't go on another day? If so, were you able to find strength? From who?

5. If you are single, how can you learn to trust God for His timing and process of sending you a mate?

Chapter 5: Turned Over

1. Did you truly turn your marriage (or desire to be married) over to the Lord?

2. Have you considered God for your decision? What are His instructions?

3. Is your health being affected by relational situations in your life? Have you taken the necessary precautions to bring healing mentally, spiritually, and physically?

4. Have you had any life changing moments? Did you hear God speak to you during it? What did He say?

5. Have you found it hard to obey God? Why or why not?

Chapter 6: Keep On, Keeping On

1. What does it mean to you to worship God?

2. Do you trust God? How can you tell?

3. Are you considering a divorce? If so, why?

4. Have you done all you can to reconcile the marriage?

5. Has God given you direction about what to do?

6. Did He ask you to remain still or did He give you a peace to depart from your marriage?

Chapter 7: Speak to the Mountain

1. Are you speaking faith-filled words or doubt and unbelief?

2. Do you talk to God about your mountain or do you talk to the mountain about your God?

3. Have you taken time to look at yourself? What do you see?

4. Are there areas in your life where you have been disobedient? If so, what are you doing to make changes?

5. Are you finding out what the Word says you should do in your situation? What does it say?

6. Have you fully decided to trust God with your situation? Are you still holding on to it or have you casted your cares to God?

Chapter 8: Porn...Be Gone!

1. Do you feel peace in your house? If not, have you found out why?

2. If you have children, are they in danger because of any addictions or issues that your spouse may have? If so, what are you doing to remove yourself and family from danger?

3. Are you refusing to change? Is your spouse refusing to change? Why?

4. Is God trying to show you the obvious? Are you paying attention or ignoring what He is showing you?

5. Can you identify the promise, process, and performance stages in your situation?

Chapter 9: A Prize Awaits

1. What prize do you believe God has waiting for you?
2. What obstacles are standing between you and the promises of God?
3. How can you attain the prize God has for you?

Chapter 10: After the Storm

1. Do you have people supporting you or are they not helpful to you?
2. If you are single, do you feel ostracized or left out? Why? If yes, what can you do to change that?
3. Do you see yourself as a victor or victim? Explain your answer.
4. Do you feel limited in ministry? Why?
5. Do you know God's plans for your life?
6. Do you believe that God can restore your life situation? Why?

Chapter 11: What Now

1. If you are engaged, do you feel like you are making a wise and God decision?
2. If you are engaged, do you feel rushed into the decision? Why?
3. How much time are you spending in the Word? Are you connected to a local church?
4. Do you have Godly people in your life who can support you?

5. What do you desire in a marriage? Do you feel like you are settling/have settled?

6. How well do you know the person you are dating/engaged to/married to? How much do you know about his or her past?

7. How well do you understand your past? Have you dealt with any issues of offensives, unforgiveness, healing?

8. Are you making it your responsibility to make him or her change?

Chapter 12: Saved Marriage

1. Are you living a life that can win someone to Christ? If not, why? If so, how?

2. How do you respond to negative behavior?

3. When your spouse looks at you, what does he see?

4. Have you sought out marital counseling for reconciliation, healing, inner strength and direction?

5. Within the last week, what have you done to demonstrate the love of God in your relationship?

6. Is it difficult for you to forgive? Why?

1. Gary Chapman, "The Marriage You've Always Wanted." Pg. 25
2. Diana Hagee, "What Every Woman Wants in a Man." Pg. 16.
3. Paula Sanford, "Healing for a Woman's Emotions."
4. Jay E. Adams, "Marriage, Divorce, and Remarriage in the Bible." Pg. 10.
5. Henry H. Halley, "Halley's Bible Handbook." Pg. 91.

Chapter 13: Saved Life

1. Is your relationship/marriage ordained by God? How can you tell?

2. Who's the first person you call in a time of need? What were the results?

3. How deep is your well? Do you believe God has the answers to your situation?

4. Do you feel alone, isolated or sometimes suicidal? If so, why? What are some ways to overcome these feelings and thoughts?

5. When was the last time you spent one on one time with God? What was your experience?

6. Do you truly believe that God loves you, and he wants you to live a victorious life?

Chapter 14: How Did I End Up Here

1. Can you think about how you got to where you are right now in life?

2. If you are divorced, do you feel like God is angry with you or has turned his back towards you? If so, why?

3. Have you accepted God's forgiveness for your past failures and mistakes?

4. Describe ways to overcome your past and embrace your future in God.

5. Are you ready to see changes in your life? Are you ready to do what it takes to see the changes?

6. How can you begin to live a life of freedom? How can you help others like you live a life of freedom?

Although, you have read the book and completed the exercise, I have one more question. Have you accepted Jesus Christ into your heart as your Lord and Personal Savior? Without Jesus, it is impossible to receive inner strength and find peace in difficult situations. If you have not accepted Jesus Christ as your Lord and Savior, I would like to take this moment to give you the opportunity to receive Him. Say this prayer aloud:

Lord, I need you in my life. I cannot live my life another day without you. Right now, _____ (today's date), I ask for forgiveness of all my sins and invite your son, Jesus Christ, to live in my heart as my Lord and Personal Savior. I will never be the same. The old things in my life have passed away and today I am a new creature in God. In Jesus Name... Amen.

APPENDIX

TESTIMONIES OF WOMEN WHO CHOSE TO LIVE

There is a woman I know today who is married to a pastor, 17 years older than her. From the beginning of their marriage, he had adulterous relationships with several women. There were many times she wanted to leave, but she could not see herself succeeding in life. During her marriage, in less than five years, she had three more children which made it a total of four children.

After they got married, he disrespected her and treated her like his child. She had to serve all of needs as if she were a slave. In return, he would not do anything for her or the children. This young lady wanted to work, but he did not allow her to work. Therefore, she barely had money to provide for her children. Sometimes, she would walk in the store with five dollars and have to decide whether to buy pampers or toilet paper. Apparently, her husband would not do right with the money. When he got paid, instead of paying the bills, he would use the money on materialistic things for himself.

As far as sexual relations, there was none. Whenever they did have sex, it was "wham, bam, thank you Ma'am." In other words, she was treated like a woman off the street or better yet, a one night stand. He had sex with her as an obligation and not as a precious gift God had given to marriage. They never became one in the spirit; married but living separate lives. Finally, she got fed up with the way he was abusing her and choose to separate.

When I asked her why she stayed in an abusive marriage for so long, her response was "I did not believe in myself, and I did not believe I could be more than I was. I did not believe I deserved better. I thought we should suffer for our consequences, and I assumed this was God's punishment for the wrong choices I made in the past. Honestly, I did not believe that God had anything better for me."

Then I went on to ask her why she married him. Her response was "I looked at his appearance, as being a pastor in the pulpit. For me, that was like heaven on earth, especially when he asked me to marry him. I thought I was chosen, and he was definitely sent by God. I did not realize that he was human like me and capable of sinning like everyone else."

Q: What gave you the courage to depart from your abusive marriage?

A: "There was a young lady who told me that it hurt her to see the way my husband was treating me. He did not acknowledge me, and he did take care of the kids. She told me that it hurt her to see me and my kids in need and my husband, who is pastor and professing to be a man of God, not help us. I began to look at the fruit in my life, and there wasn't any.

Since the beginning of my marriage, he has lied and I had caught him several times cheating on me. He treated me like his slave, and he did not spend time with the children. Every time we turned around we were being evicted out of an apartment or a house. He would smoke illegal drugs and do other things that were not right. At the same time, he would go to the church and preach a sermon like everything was cool.

Recently, I caught him again with a woman who lived next to the church, hugging and kissing on her. When I begin to look over my life, I did not see any fruit in his life or in my life. I knew then it was time to go. I had already been praying and asking God for direction. Now, He has provided my answer. God had given me a peace to leave."

Q: What would you tell other women who are in an abusive relationship and afraid to leave?

A: "God did not call you to suffer. He called you to an abundant life. If you are contemplating whether you should leave or not, I suggest you pray first. Always pray and follow the leading of the Holy Spirit. He will lead you into all truth (everything you desire to know). Additionally, look at the fruit in your marriage and in your life, then pray and ask God to reveal to you His purpose. Through prayer, God will answer your cry."

Q: What advice do you have for singles that are waiting for a mate?

A: "Wait on God and choose God's best. It gets hard and we rush, but you must wait to avoid resentment and heart aching pain. Sometimes we see other people's relationships and desire to have a marriage like theirs. In most cases, you are looking at the surface and do not know exactly what goes on behind closed doors. "Do not believe the hype."

The best advice I can give to you is to nurture your relationship with God and believe in who you are in Christ. You have to know who you are in Christ and have self assurance and confidence that you are complete in Christ. Therefore, you will not have to look for a man or woman to complete you. "For in Christ dwelleth all the fullness of the Godhead bodily. And ye are complete in him, which is the head of all principality and power (Colossians 2:9-10, emphasis added).

Everything you need is in Christ and in Him alone. Remember just because they are in the church does not mean the church is on the inside of them. Do not judge the book by its cover. You have to peel back the onion and see if it is what God has for you. I thought since my husband was a preacher there was no sin in him. I put him on a pedestal. I failed to realize that regardless of a person's credentials or status, they still have the same human tendency, struggles and appetite everyone else does. Therefore, pray, pray, and pray until God confirms your perfect mate."

Testimony: "God gave me hope. He restored my ambition, my drive, and my passion for living. Although, I'm tired from working two jobs to provide for my kids, just to wake up each day in freedom is a wonderful and peaceful thing. I would not trade my liberty for anything in this world. Even though it is not quite how I want it to be, I still have peace and the satisfaction that God is going to make a way. I just have to take one step at a time. Since I've been separated from my husband, I have not gone without anything. I came from a marriage where there was always lack. There were times I only had $5 in my pocket, and I had to make a decision to buy pampers or toilet paper. Now, I can walk in the store and buy the things I need for myself and my children. I've come from a position of lack to now being sustained by God. It makes me appreciate the small things and what God has in store for me that is out of this world. At first, I thought I could not do anything with my life. Now, there is a freedom that I can do all things through Jesus Christ who gives me strength everyday."

Take a Stand

Whether you are married or not, God does not desire for you to live in an abusive relationship. Paula Sandford talks about a young lady in her book, *Healing for a Woman's Emotions*, who was in a common law marriage for many years. Facing pain (mother left when she was two years old and her father was violent and an alcoholic) in her own life as a teenager, she was drawn to a man not too far from her home. Eventually, she moved away with this guy, only to find out later he was abusive like her father. As the years went on, he drank excessively and became more and more abusive. While living with him, she had two daughters. Similar to my situation, this woman became fearful for her two daughters.

When she met this guy, she did not know the Lord. Soon this woman found a church home and established a relationship with the Lord. "Over a period of time, she gained enough inner strength and self-esteem to stand up and say "no" to her common law-husband, and she left him. She studied to earn her GED and did a creditable job of struggling to provide a home for her girls. There was never enough money to cover all their physical needs, but there seemed to be much more safety in poverty than she had known in the relationship from which she had fled" (Sandford, 169 - 170).

This message is true and dear to my heart. It hurts for me to see anyone in this situation. It took this woman over 18 years to rise above her circumstances (abuse) and trust God as her provider. Although, it took her 18 years, she is still a conqueror. She chose to live in freedom.

I was a victim, but today I live as a victor. All the lies that the enemy has put before you, is exactly what it is: a lie. Every lie he told me about my ministry and my success has come to naught (fell on stony grounds).

You can live. I'm a living testimony, along with the other testimonies. At times, I felt ashamed for having a child. I felt like my life was shot, and I did not want to live. It was so bad when I looked up I saw the ground. That's just how far down my life was. I was in a rut.

But look at me today. God has brought me through a tough situation and showed me a life of purpose which is living for Him and not for a man. "For in him we live, and move, and have our being" (Acts 17:28). Now, I'm able to live and move and do the things God has called me to do.

As I mentioned before, I am more successful than I had ever been and have gone further in my ministry and in my own personal life. I thank God for my new freedom in Him.

If you are the one sheep that is separated from the other 99, God has sent me on His behalf to bring you back to Him. He wants you to know, "There is HOPE." God will provide. Do not look at the impossible. "If thou canst believe, all things are possible to him that believeth" (Mark 9:23). He will make a way when it seems like there is no way and all hope is gone.

So HOLD your head up HIGH, and KNOW that you are a child of the Most High God!

To correspond with Sabrina Barfield, order books,
or for more information on booking her for a
speaking engagement, you may write her:

strongtowermin@yahoo.com
Or
log on to her website at
www.sabrinabarfield.com
www.strongtoweroutreach.com

CPSIA information can be obtained at www.ICGtesting.com
Printed in the USA
LVOW111855090512

281069LV00020B/110/P